Simplicity Rules

Teaching: the best job in the world. Yet, increasingly, it is considered one of the toughest professions. In recent years, practices have arisen and become widespread which overcomplicate teaching and increase teacher workload, while only having a marginal impact on pupil learning. *Simplicity Rules* explores how children learn and the most effective ways to teach them, focusing on achieving results using strategies that are low effort and high impact, along with a comprehensive framework underpinning the ideas.

Covering what to teach, talk, practice, starting a lesson, ending a lesson, and feedback alongside practical methods to reduce workload as well as simpler and clearer systems to support teachers in the long term, this book asks:

- Is this the very best use of my time as a teacher?

- What is the learning impact for the child?

- What is the impact on my own workload?

- Are the results worth this effort?

Promoting a simplification of teaching practices, *Simplicity Rules* is an essential guide for school teachers of all levels of experience, and school leaders.

Jo Facer is Vice Principal at The Ebbsfleet Academy, UK. She tweets @jo_facer and blogs at readingallthebooks.com.

Simplicity Rules

How Simplifying What We Do in the Classroom Can Benefit Children

Jo Facer

LONDON AND NEW YORK

First published 2019
by Routledge
2 Park Square, Milton Park, Abingdon, Oxon, OX14 4RN

and by Routledge
52 Vanderbilt Avenue, New York, NY 10017

Routledge is an imprint of the Taylor & Francis Group, an informa business

British Library Cataloguing-in-Publication Data
A catalogue record for this book is available from the British Library

Library of Congress Cataloging-in-Publication Data
Names: Facer, Jo, editor.
Title: Simplicity rules : how simplifying what we do can benefit children /
    Jo Facer.
Description: Abingdon, Oxon ; New York, NY : Routledge, 2019. |
    Includes bibliographical references.
Identifiers: LCCN 2018059791 | ISBN 9781138488632 (hbk) |
    ISBN 9781138488649 (pbk) | ISBN 9781351039789 (ebk)
Subjects: LCSH: Teaching—Methodology. | Effective teaching. |
    Learning, Psychology of.
Classification: LCC LB1025.3 .F34 2019 | DDC 371.102—dc23
LC record available at https://lccn.loc.gov/2018059791

ISBN: 978-1-138-48863-2 (hbk)
ISBN: 978-1-138-48864-9 (pbk)
ISBN: 978-1-351-03978-9 (ebk)

Typeset in Melior
by Apex CoVantage, LLC

Visit the eResources: www.routledge.com/9781138488649

Contents

Introduction

Teaching is inherently complex. The idea of presenting for an hour to 30 people six times a day would flummox most people in business; yet teachers handle this complexity day in, day out. Just the act of teaching a single lesson – let alone a full day of them – is complex in the extreme.

In any given classroom, a teacher might have up to 32 students, each with different experiences, temperaments, cultural capital, abilities, emotions, literacy levels, and attitudes to learning. Each child has a unique relationship not only with their teacher, but also with the other 31 students in the class; these relationships can change their behaviour and impede or progress their learning, and, as teachers, we can't control most of them.

So I'm not trying to say that teaching is simple.

But what I have noticed over the past eight years in the classroom is that we often needlessly add layers of complexity through our practice. This is unhelpful for two reasons.

Firstly, the experience of school from the child's perspective. For children, they too experience school as an extremely complex institution. In their six-period day, they might have six different subjects exposing them to new ideas, new concepts, and new areas that they need to make sense of. In each lesson, they might see different teachers, with whom their interactions are marked by differing expectations to understand. The buzzword of one school I worked in was 'consistency,' and I think children deserve as much consistency as we can give them. The more complexity, the less likely it will be to reach consistency.

Secondly, teacher workload increases as complexity in the classroom increases. We know that our profession is haemorrhaging teachers, teachers we cannot easily replace.[1] We can't afford – financially or ethically – to keep replacing good people leaving the profession because they wanted ordinary things; things like a family, or a free evening, or a weekend without work. The more we make our practice complex, the more we add to our own workload.

In this book, I hope to reveal another way. If we can scrap complexity from every part of teaching in our control, we can both cut our workload and ensure our students have an enhanced experience of school: learning more, achieving more and, as a result, ensuring they enjoy more choices in their future.

Starting with the science of how children learn, we explore how to maximise student learning while not maximising our workloads. The second chapter considers behaviour, and how a simpler system can lead to improved student behaviour. In Chapter 3, we consider how we might simplify what we teach, and in Chapter 4 the resources we use. The key lesson practices advocated are explored in Chapters 6 to 9: reading, writing, discussing, and independent practice. Finally, Chapter 11 considers how we can feed back to students in a simpler way.

There is a simpler, easier way out there. I believe that the more we move towards it, the easier and happier the lives of both teachers and pupils will be.

Note

1 The *Guardian* reported that just under 40,000 teachers left the profession in 2016 – approximately 9% of the workforce. www.theguardian.com/education/2018/may/13/teacher-burnout-shortages-recruitment-problems-budget-cuts

How children learn

It makes sense, before we dive into exploring how to teach simply, to recall what we know from scientific and educational research about how children learn. Evidently, we need to ensure we teach the requisite content knowledge and that children understand it. We look at the best ways to ensure learning is memorable, and touch on some factors which might impact on the memorability of the content, such as cultural literacy.

Knowledge or skills

What does it mean to have 'learned' something? At its most basic, we tend to think of learning as leading to being able to do something we couldn't previously. This is clearest at primary level, when children go from not being able to read to being able to read; not being able to write to writing. As children grow older, this concept becomes more and more contentious. When children can *already* read and write, what does it mean to 'read better' or 'write better'? For the former, it might be argued that reading age tests can guide us, but anyone who has given these, even to year 7 children, will attest to the difficulty of 11-year-olds 'capping out' the test: reaching the highest 'reading age' already. And what about every other subject?

In education, currently two broad camps exist. One camp says learning means children have mastered a skill. The other says children have mastered components of knowledge.

Knowledge

Mastering a skill makes sense when we are talking about art, design, and technology practical work, and sports. But how do we teach the 'skill' of 'analysis'?

A few years ago, a teacher I worked with told me about a pupil who wanted to know how to get better at history. He showed him his history book, wherein was inscribed his teacher's feedback: 'You need more analysis.' And yet my colleague's response on questioning the child on that particular historical period was 'you don't know enough about these events. So how can you possibly analyse it?' The feedback was not helpful, because to analyse more he needed to know more. And children, like anyone, cannot know what they don't know.

The opposing view to 'skills,' if the two can really be said to be 'opposing' at all, is that learning means mastering knowledge components. We can tell if a child has learned a fact, because we teach them the square root of nine in today's lesson, and we see if they still know it tomorrow. We teach them that the Battle of Hastings was in 1066, and see if they still know that in their final assessment. But these isolated facts are nowhere near enough. Whether or not a child can write does not solely depend on how many facts they have learned.

Even if you are committed to the idea that learning is all about skills, it can still be helpful to consider learning as 'knowledge based.' This is because breaking down 'skills' *into* knowledge components makes them easier to teach. As an English teacher, when I read my pupils' books, I can see that their writing would be improved if they wrote more fluently. But to guide them to write more fluently, it would help if I broke down that advice into knowledge components. For my lowest-achieving pupils, they need to know that sentences begin with capital letters and end with full stops. They need to know that paragraphs are made up of sentences, each of which should contain a complete thought, and that each paragraph should be focused on one idea. They need to know how to embed quotations. They need to know some words, and what those words mean, before they can string them into a sentence.

Cognitive scientists would add a crucial caveat to the foregoing. They would add that 'if nothing has changed in long-term memory, nothing has been learned.'[1] If I know when the Battle of Hastings was today, but I don't know it in two weeks' time, can I really be said to have 'learned' that isolated fact? We can all think back to our GCSEs and wonder how on earth we managed that top grade in French although we can't speak a word, or that top grade in chemistry even though we can't even remember the chemical symbol for the most basic of elements. Is knowing it 'at some point' really enough?

Understanding

As teachers, thankfully we aren't directly responsible for what our children remember when they are 35-year-old professionals. We often use their results at key tests to determine how well they have 'learned.' But, as we explore later, success in these tests is not solely determined by how well we drill children in the specification.

Before we concern ourselves with memory, there is an earlier stage to the mystery of learning. For children to learn, they must understand what we are teaching them.

The biggest argument against 'knowledge led' teaching is that it leads to children parroting lists of facts with no understanding of what they are saying. (I often think of this view sympathetically when I hear primary school–age pupils rapping songs that are currently playing on 'young people's' radio stations: they 'know' all the words, but, thank goodness, they really have no idea of what those words mean. A colleague of mine a few years back stopped a year 7 who was singing Jason Derulo's 2013 'Talk Dirty to Me' and asked the girl what it meant to 'talk dirty.' The girl blushed, giggled, and said: 'I think it's about . . . poo!')

Rote learning can be argued to have a place in learning, albeit a limited one. In the very earliest stages of language learning, it can be helpful to simply learn the translation of vocabulary, even without a detailed understanding of how to combine those words into a sentence, because, well, you have to start somewhere, and at some point you simply need to know that the Latin word for 'table' is, forgettably, 'mensa.' There isn't really an easy trick to that – the two words look completely different, and unless your teacher is some kind of magician who can think of a handy trick to help you remember each and every word in the language, you really just have to learn it. In maths, if you learn all of your times tables off by heart, you will have an excellent base from which to further manipulate numbers. But in both cases, rote knowledge of times tables or frequently occurring words won't get you very far.

Questioning

Children must, as the absolute baseline of learning, understand what we are teaching them. If they have not understood what every word and concept means, having it in the memory to reel out on command is meaningless. This is exemplified by a comment by a Reddit user, who when told 'knowledge is power: Francis Bacon,' with limited knowledge heard this as 'knowledge is power: France is bacon.' They struggled to understand the second part of the phrase, but recited it for years and saw people nodding in agreement, only to have the penny drop years later when they finally saw it written down.[2] How many children are out there right now, able to reel off dates and quotes, without actually knowing what they are saying? Rote learning is beguilingly easy when children are receptive. We have to spend time ensuring pupils understand what they are learning *first*.

Which is why I would go as far as to say: the most important part of pedagogy that every teacher must master is the art of *questioning*. How do we know whether children understand what we are teaching them? We need to ask them.

The problem is, it is remarkably difficult to know the right questions to ask to ensure every pupil has accurately understood the topic being taught in all its nuance. Moreover, we are dealing with up to 34 children at a time, which complicates matters. Although some schools would like to believe that a single 'hinge question' that all pupils answer will give the teacher the required data to know whether they have 'got it,' the content of our lessons is rarely simple enough to be assessed accurately by one magical question. (I once worked in a school that tried to include this: at the halfway point of a lesson, teachers had to ask one question and have a whole-class response to judge whether pupils were on track to understand the lesson. This may be fine if the sole content of your lesson is 'know what a simile is,' but it is rather more challenging when you have to also read and understand Chapter 3 of *Oliver Twist* in all its complexity.)

So, I would say, questioning is about knowing the *multiple* questions you will ask of the *multiple* children in your class. Indeed, I would go so far as to argue that the best preparation a teacher can do for their lesson is to *script their questions*. This is as easy as taking the lesson content – be it a worksheet, textbook, or novel chapter – and annotating it, not with our ideas but with our questions. Beside a passage revealing the plight of the poor workhouse boys in *Oliver Twist*, then, you would not write 'poverty displayed' but instead 'What does Dickens reveal about the workhouse boys?' You might then write 'Which words tell us this?' Alternatively, if your class already comprehends the material, you might write '*How* does Dickens display their poverty?' or 'How does Dickens make the reader feel sympathy?'

This may sound simple – and I hope that almost all of the advice in this book is simple – but it is probably the most complex aspect of teaching. To know which questions to ask, you need to know: what are the key points you want students to understand? What are the misconceptions they may have over an aspect of the learning? What does the class as a whole struggle with? What do individual students in the class struggle with? What questions can ensure they are practising the things they most frequently struggle with? At root, effective questioning requires a deep knowledge of the curriculum content combined with a deep knowledge of the pupils in the class.

That is why I say again that the most effective planning a teacher can do is to know the content of the lesson, work out what the children will struggle with, and work out how they will know the children have understood it. The teacher then needs to script questions that will clarify confusions, highlight key ideas, and give them information on who 'gets it' and who does not.

How to question a class

The practice of questioning has attracted some debate over the past several years. How do we decide who to ask questions of? Clearly, if we solely rely on asking pupils who put their hands up we will end up with a number of 'false positives,' whereby we wishfully imagine the keen pupil who has readily given the right answer represents the average level of learning of all pupils, including those hiding from our questioning gaze, hoping they won't be asked. If we only ask the very keenest and most confident children for their responses, and their responses are correct, we might move on with our lesson far too rapidly, not realising that perhaps two thirds of the class are being left behind.

Some in education have advocated 'hands down questioning,' meaning that students are instructed to never raise their hands, and teachers always choose who answers their questions. The major benefit of hands down questioning is that because teachers always choose who answers each question, all pupils must be always ready to respond. For every question the teacher asks, every pupil must be thinking of their answer. If teachers only ask for hands up, then pupils might easily think: 'oh, I'm tired and that's a tough question. I'll sit this one out and start focusing next time.'

While hands down questioning is good to keep all pupils on their toes, I would advise teachers against 'random name generators' or 'lolly sticks' with pupils' names on them. Why? Sometimes you ask a question of the whole class, but you particularly want one pupil to answer it. Maybe it's a pupil who has really struggled with this idea in the past. Maybe it's a pupil who missed a lesson last week and you're checking they understand as they've had less subject instruction than others. Maybe it's a pupil who is often lazy. Maybe it's a pupil who is often disruptive of your lesson and needs a 'win,' and you know they know the answer to this one (more on behaviour management in Chapter 2). There are a myriad of reasons you might want to have a particular pupil answer a particular question: don't deny yourself the right to choose the pupil.

At the same time, I have become a recent convert to 'hands up' questioning. Hands up gives us some important data: who is engaged in the learning? Who wants to try answering the difficult questions? Who *thinks* they understand at this moment in time? When you ask a question and get a sea of hands in the air, that may mean the pitch of the lesson is too low – although it is not necessarily a bad thing to have every pupil knowing the answer at least some of the time, particularly for core concepts you want them to 'overlearn.'[3] More importantly, if you ask a question and no one, or almost no one, puts their hand up, you know you need to re-explain.

Just because you allow hands up does not mean you can't suddenly ask a question of a pupil with their hand down. You, after all, are the teacher, the one who makes all the decisions in your classroom. That said, if you only take pupils with their hands down, the others will swiftly stop bothering to put their hands up – 'what's the point? Miss is more likely to call on me if I keep my hand down.' You need to judge it. I like to mix it up, perhaps with a class where most pupils put their hands up taking five hands up for every 'cold call' of a kid with their hand down, depending on the particular question I am asking and the particular child I want to ask.

With a class who are reluctant to put their hands up – in my experience, older pupils in lower attaining groupings – I rarely use hands up questions as too few pupils participate for this to work. I will often narrate: 'hands down – I'm going to decide who is answering,' for the benefit of the two in 20 who actually do wish to put their hands up.

Improving how we ask questions is one of the best areas we can place our professional development efforts. If you're lucky enough to have someone who comes and observes you regularly, ask them for feedback on which questions worked well and which did not. A question which works well is one which consolidates learning, checks understanding, moves the lesson on, probes understanding, or pre-empts a misconception. A question that doesn't work is one which is usually pitched incorrectly: stupidly easy, and everyone knows the answer, or stupidly difficult and no one does.

Memory

After pupils have understood the content of a lesson, the next stage is to commit that content to memory. We are lucky that such extensive research by cognitive scientists has already been undertaken on how memory works. A number of key facts about memory are pertinent to teaching. These are: short-term memory is easily overloaded, long-term memory is practically limitless, we forget things if we aren't reminded of them, and we remember things better if they make sense to us in the context of the other things we already remember.

Although research on the precise number varies, it is generally asserted that we can hold between three and as many as seven new ideas in our short-term memory.[4] Any more, and we become overloaded and simply cannot make sense of the ideas. This helps to explain why mixed-ability teaching is so difficult: the teacher may feel they are only introducing one or two 'new' concepts, but if a struggling learner has yet to comprehend the language of the learning, or master what we might discount as 'simple things' (like where to use capital letters and full stops), then to them we are actually introducing a much wider range of 'new' ideas and they simply cannot keep up.

On the other hand, our long-term memories are so capacious as to be basically limitless for practically all humans going through schooling. We don't need to worry about children forgetting one thing once they learn another *if* the first is *properly* committed to long-term memory. Once it's stuck in there, you're good to go.

The problem is that we as educators often confuse 'I taught it' with 'they learned it.'[5] We are frustrated when the class comes to us two days after we have done an entire beautifully planned lesson on similes, and literally no one can tell us what a simile is. This problem is partly the expert-novice issue: as experts, we can't always empathise with children who find our subject challenging. We can do long multiplication; how can they not add two and two together? It is hard to put ourselves in the mindset of the novice learner, and we are constantly underestimating what *we* know and overestimating what the children know.[6] In reality, we have acquired our long-term memory of key subject facts over a long time, and through multiple exposures to these ideas. It is reckoned that children need to be exposed to a new idea at least four times for it to stick.[7] We need, therefore, to keep referring back to the new material we teach far more than we think we do. The beauty of the concept of 'overlearning,' though, is that you can never teach something too many times. 'Overlearning' is just the process of going over and over what is being learned. At one school I worked in, teachers used to say that kids should revise 'not until you *nearly* know it, but until you *really* know it.'

The final point to bear in mind about memory is that learning facts in isolation is extremely difficult. When we first hear new facts, we make sense of them in connection to other facts we know: our minds construct a schema of ideas.[8] This is why we need to think very carefully about the order in which we teach children new ideas: they will be making sense of what we teach by connecting it to what they already know.

Learning the basics of a subject off by heart is crucial to a pupil's future success in that subject. In maths, knowing number bonds and times tables in a pupil's long-term memory means that working memory can be freed up to focus on new maths ideas, which often rely on pupils' basic understanding of numbers. In English, knowing punctuation and sentence structure will similarly free pupils' working memories to focus on new ideas in analysis or creating their own stories.

Make it memorable

So, how can teachers make their lessons memorable? Daniel Willingham provides a number of suggestions in *Why Don't Students Like School?* He writes that 'memory . . . is a product of what you think about.'[9] We therefore need to ensure our pupils are spending the lesson thinking about what we want them to remember. This means cutting out distracting and superfluous activities and digressions, entertaining as these may be for pupils and teachers alike. The second piece of advice from Willingham is to make new learning like a story: we have developed an excellent ability to understand and remember stories with relatively little effort. This is tricky to do.[10] The third piece of advice is easier for all teachers: go over the material again. And again. And again. In fact, the easiest way to make children remember something is to test them on it – the subject of a later chapter in this book. Put in its simplest way, though, the best way to check if children are remembering what we have taught them is to ask them.

Asking questions, as I've already said, is the most important thing we do as teachers. In Chapters 5 and 8, I go into more detail on the questions we ask of whom and how. Briefly, we can insert more questions into our lessons to test our pupils' memories by starting our lessons with recaps of previous lessons. We should periodically use questions to test pupils' memories of previous material. It is important that we have isolated the key material we want our pupils to remember, however; otherwise such questioning is meaningless. I too have been guilty of asking pupils 'how many marks is question 3, and how long do you need to spend on it?' Of course, in the run-up to a major exam, such questions have their place. But they are nowhere near as important as the questions we ask children when they are in the process of learning powerful knowledge.

If we have broken down what we want pupils to know, we then need to regularly check they know it. How quickly children commit an idea to long-term memory is not an exact science; although I would argue that pupils have more in common in terms of how they learn than differences, they definitely differ in the length of time it takes for them to retain ideas. If you see your pupils every day, why not include a weekly quiz to quickly see how much of the learning that week pupils have retained? You can ask four questions of the learning of that week, and add one 'wildcard' question throwing back to previous learning. As the unit goes on, you might want to extend this quiz or throw in a greater proportion of questions on prior learning. I would keep the quiz to under ten questions if possible, however; more than that and you will spend too great a proportion of learning time 'weighing the pig,' perhaps at the expense of teaching wider curriculum content or reinforcing key skills pupils need time to practise in your subject.

Multiple-choice questions

One way that has gained some traction in testing pupil learning in recent years is to curate multiple-choice questions. I was first converted to these when hearing Daisy Christodoulou sing their praises a number of years ago. There are huge benefits to using multiple-choice questions. Firstly, pupils need to read the question and the possible answers, and then pick one possible answer. This is far quicker than asking pupils to write their answer. Secondly, there is then a definitive right or wrong answer, something you don't usually get with 'free writing.' The speed with which you can mark these improves also, as you won't have hands up as pupils check the *precise* wording they have individually chosen to answer the question. Finally, and perhaps most importantly, you can include in the 'distractor' answers (the wrong ones) some classic misconceptions. For example, pupils may not remember that Macbeth is 'Thane of Glamis' at the outset of the play. So, if you ask pupils, 'What is Macbeth's title at the start of the play?' you might include distractors like 'King;' 'Thane of Cawdor,' or 'He doesn't have one.' Pupils choosing any of these three display that they have not yet learned exactly the timeline of Macbeth's many titles, which means they have also not fully understood some key plot points. You as the teacher then know you need to go over and clarify these key points.

There are, however, some drawbacks to using multiple-choice questions. The most obvious concern teachers have is: what if pupils are just guessing? And that is problematic. If you only give students a choice of two answers, perhaps in a 'true or false' style, a pupil who has no idea but simply guesses still has a 50% chance of being correct. This is improved with added options; I would suggest four to five is optimal, to ensure pupils aren't able to just blindly guess. Any more options than five, and the test will begin to take a long time, especially for pupils who read slowly.

The other concern teachers have is that these questions take a long time to create. That is true, and unfortunately I don't have any response to that, except to say that they are transferrable. One teacher who makes them for their one class can readily hand them out to all teachers of the same department. One teacher who makes them for one class one year can also reuse them the following year.

When I write multiple-choice questions, I begin with the question and the answer. Once I can see the question and the answer for all five, or all ten, that I am writing, I begin to work on the distractors. When I write a distractor, I try to think: 'what mistakes could be easily made when answering this question?' If you're an inexperienced teacher, this is much more challenging, as a lot of knowing what children struggle with comes from experience in the classroom. If you're unable to work out what children struggle with, you might simply change character names, or dates. The closer together your answers are, the harder it will be for pupils. ('When was the Battle of Hastings?' 'a) 1466 b) 1266 c) 1366 d) 1066 e) 1166.') Another easy win is to use your knowledge grid (more on these in Chapter 4), and ask the same question but mix up the responses. So, in a grid with character names and traits, you would simply write: 'Who is the overly ambitious man who kills the king?' 'a) Lady Macbeth b) Duncan c) Macbeth d) Thane of Cawdor e) Banquo.'

If I were a new teacher struggling for time, I would jettison multiple-choice questions in favour of more open-answer questions. These are quick to write and relatively easy to assess, notwithstanding clarifying questions from your pupils. But if you have some time to invest in creating resources – perhaps you're in a well-resourced department, looking to improve how you ensure pupils' understanding of key concepts – then I think multiple-choice questions are a really good thing to spend your time on.

Cultural literacy

The question that has been plaguing educators for some time now has no easy answer: why is it that children from poorer backgrounds tend to find learning more difficult?

Many books have been written on the sociology of deprivation, and it is beyond doubt that children who grow up in poverty experience tough emotional challenges.

It is also obvious that children who grow up with middle-class families who are educated to a high standard, have high expectations for what their children can and should achieve, and (crucially, I think), *know how to get them there*, will have an advantage. What do those parents know how to do? They know how important reading is for children, for example. They can know without 'knowing' how important conversation is over dinner each night. They know which museums to take their children to, and they usually know something about what is shown in a museum to help to explain what their children are looking at. Try as I might, I can't think of a way to imbue new parents from poor educational backgrounds with enough tacit knowledge to be able to do what middle-class parents seem to do without even thinking about it (and even if I had a way, the logistics of teaching this would prove impossible).

By the time children from disadvantaged backgrounds come to us in secondary school, there are often so many gaps in their knowledge it is hard to know where to begin. That's not because primary schools don't do an excellent job. It's just that what children need to know to be able to compete with their wealthier peers is staggering. I visited Eton College a number of years ago and remember reading a 'bottom set' year 9 boy's essay on poetry that was so complex and mature it outpaced any sixth formers I had taught. Can we ever close that gap?

Perhaps not in schools. Perhaps seven years of secondary school and six years of primary school is not enough time. But if we can give children enough knowledge to pass those crucial exams, get into those good universities, and (here's the kicker) *have a genuine love of learning*, then of course that gap will close. There are plenty of leading lights in academia, politics, medicine and so on, who went to mediocre, or even terrible, schools. What we need to do for children from more deprived backgrounds is to ensure they learn as much as they can, as fast as they can, enough so they can get to our best institutions of higher education. Along the way, we need to awaken in them the thirst for knowledge, so that they will continue to work hard and learn and explore academically all their lives.

I write this here because I think it is important to clarify what we are doing in schools. For very many children, school is the only place that will change the course of their lives. To serve the children of our more deprived communities best means not only giving them a diet of the 'best that has been thought and said.' If we did only that, we may risk teaching children too broadly, and they may not pass those crucial exams. But if we only drill children to pass exams, they may fall down at the next hurdle in their education – something I go into more in Chapter 3. And if we only teach children powerful knowledge and how to pass exams, then paradoxically we may turn them off learning for life and they will never catch up.

So, what do we need to do in schools? We need to teach children quality knowledge, which enables them to pass exams to a high standard, while making them excited about learning in a way that will stay with them for their whole lives.

So, where do we begin? I suggest beginning somewhere that actually has nothing to do with cultural literacy, or what we teach children. I suggest beginning with behaviour.

Put simply

- Instead of making a beautiful PowerPoint, or worrying about a mix of activities, prepare to teach by writing the questions you will ask the class on the reading they will do.

- Instead of making lolly sticks, or sourcing random name generators, ask a lot of questions in your lesson.

- Instead of cramming in as many new ideas as possible, continually retest the core ideas to check the students *really* know them.

Notes

1 'Why Minimal Guidance During Instruction Does Not Work: An Analysis of the Failure of Constructivist, Discovery, Problem-Based, Experiential, and Inquiry-Based Teaching': Kirschner, Sweller and Clarke. www.cogtech.usc.edu/publications/kirschner_Sweller_Clark.pdf

2 www.reddit.com/r/AskReddit/comments/dxosj/what_word_or_phrase_did_you_totally_misunderstand/

3 'Instead of practicing until you're decent at something and then taking a siesta, practicing just a little longer could be the fast track to solidifying a skill. "Overlearning" is the process of rehearsing a skill even after you no longer improve.' www.scientificamerican.com/article/the-power-of-overlearning/ Accessed 15.9.18

4 In *Seven Myths About Education*, Daisy Christodoulou writes: 'There is some debate in the literature about exactly how limited working memory is, but some of the most recent research suggests that it may be limited to as few as three or four items,' p. 18 (Routledge 2014); a number of journal articles do suggest seven or eight are possible.

5 Doug Lemov, *Teach Like a Champion 2.0*: 'John Wooden . . . once said the most crucial task of teaching was to distinguish "I taught it" from "they learned it",' p. 18 (Jossey Bass 2015).

6 Christodoulou notes: 'I think that many educated people underestimate how much knowledge they have, and overestimate how much knowledge children have,' p. 83 (*Seven Myths About Education*).

7 'Most research states that the average student needs at least four exposures to something to add it to his/her knowledge base.' *A Practical Guide to Teaching and Learning*, Oran Tkatchov and Michele Pollnow, p. 25 (R&L Education 2011).

8 In *Curious*, Ian Leslie writes: 'New knowledge is assimilated better, and has more creative possibility, the bigger the store of existing knowledge it is joining. Knowledge loves knowledge.' (Quercus 2015)

9 *Why Don't Students Like School*, Daniel T. Willingham, p. 53.

10 Tricky, but not impossible. One of my current colleagues has the knack of making everything he teaches a memorable story. We are still trying to work out how he does it. If I find out, I'll give you the answer. I suspect it is rather simple though: he's been doing this a very long time, and he knows an awful lot about the subject.

2 Good behaviour

The first, and most important, factor in whether a lesson succeeds is down to one thing: how well the children behave. If children are poorly behaved, it does not matter whether you are teaching the best lesson ever written and delivered in all of human history. No one will learn. Or, no one will learn as much as they could and should. Ensuring pupils behave is the most important job of any teacher.

What is good behaviour?

Our ideas about what constitutes 'good' behaviour, though, may need some calibrating. What we expect children to be able to do, and how we expect them to control themselves, will have an obvious impact on how high the standards in our classrooms are. What we think of as good behaviour is formed by our experience: both by the schools we went to and by the schools we have worked in. In this chapter, we consider teacher expectations of behaviour, how to work with your particular school context, what to do when your school does not have a behaviour policy (as is reported to be the case in a concerning number of educational establishments), and what I think a great school's behaviour policy looks like.

Why is good behaviour central to good learning? Two reasons. First, and most obviously, if pupils are not behaving, they are not listening to what you are teaching them. So, if they talk when you talk, or even whisper, they miss out on key learning. If they talk instead of writing, they miss out on practising what they have learned. If they talk instead of reading, they read less than their counterparts who are focused on the reading, and so perpetuate being behind their peers. I mention talking and whispering because in every school I have worked in or visited, this is the most common behaviour that slows down learning. The 'big ticket items,' like shouting, swearing, and throwing things, obviously not only stop the individual learning, but they also stop the rest of the class from learning because the teacher cannot both teach and deal with these. Thankfully, these kinds of behaviours are far less prevalent than 'low level disruption.'

The second reason that good behaviour is central to good learning is because schools teach more than just subjects. Schools also teach children how to be good people. In society, we don't get very far if we are rude, if we talk back, if we talk over others, if we don't listen, if we don't focus. In schools we need to escape the idea that teaching children how to behave is teaching them 'obedience,' a word which, for many, has connotations of oppression and fear. We aren't teaching that at all. We are teaching children how to be polite. Just as in a university lecture, or a cinema or theatre, it wouldn't work if everyone was having a chat with their mate, so in a classroom the polite behaviour is to listen to the adult talking, or the peer talking when directed by the person in charge of the classroom, the teacher.

Obedience

Some people find the idea of children being 'obedient' challenging to accept. Our understanding of modern history plays into this fear: in a world where unquestioning acceptance has resulted in mass slaughter of a people in all corners of the globe, we are understandably uneasy about the idea of children unquestioningly accepting our every word. Yet, we should think of this less in terms of 'unquestioning acceptance' and more in terms of 'social norms.' If we taught children one on one, the learning would of course be dialogic and pushback would be fine. A child asking 'why this rule?' could have the answer put to them immediately, and any learning lost would be that child's and that child's alone.

But in a classroom of 32 children, pushback and questioning teacher authority results in chaos – quite literally in some of our weakest schools. The classroom's success relies on children complying with social norms. This does not mean they cannot push back *intellectually*, of course. In my classroom, children can't call out, or leave their seats and wander around, or distract their peers. But they are welcomed, and even encouraged, in saying: 'I disagree with that interpretation,' when I teach them a poem.

The wider reality we have to face is that good behaviour in a classroom is a necessary precursor to success in life. The children who argue back and who are rude to their teachers are not going to magically transform themselves into prime candidates for the best jobs, or for future promotions. Children may very well say, and I have been told this by many a cocky teenager, 'I'd listen to my boss because they pay my wages.' But the reality is that our everyday actions form our character: as Durant says, 'we are what we repeatedly do.'[1] The habits we enact each day form the people we become.

A well-ordered classroom

So, now we're clear we're not going to oppress anyone by making them be polite, let's start by outlining what 'good behaviour' looks like. In a well-ordered classroom, children will all be sitting where the teacher has told them to sit (first time, without argument). They will have their equipment on the desk, ready to use it – not in their bags, where they have to scrabble around to retrieve it before a task begins. They will keep their hands to themselves. They will focus on the lesson, not doodling or writing notes, or whispering to their peers. Focusing on the lesson means looking towards the teacher, or the board, or the textbook, or their exercise book. They will not be looking out of the window and daydreaming. When the teacher asks a question, they will raise their hands to contribute; and if they are not chosen, they will accept the teacher's decision and put their hands down.

In a well-ordered classroom, when a teacher gives an instruction, children will follow it, first time, and without undue pausing, questioning, or argument. They will complete tasks without deliberately wasting time. If a teacher reminds a pupil of the classroom expectations, the pupil will either apologise or say nothing, and in both cases will change their behaviour. Pupils will do nothing to distract their peers – no foot tapping, pen clicking, silly answers, silly noises.

The ground rules

Good behaviour boils down to two clear ground rules:

1 The pupils follow the teacher's instructions first time, every time.

2 The pupils focus 100% on learning.

Every other suggested rule stems from these two ground rules.

But sadly, it is not as simple as that. Because some pupils will not, I'm afraid, follow the teacher's instructions, certainly not every time, and often not the first time, and, being young people in a world of technology, gossip, and short-term pleasures (and, frankly, being *people*) their natural focus is likely *not* to be on what we are teaching. Unless you are very, very lucky, that is. (I have been amazed at the similar levels of disinterest in learning between the most impoverished children at a local school and the wealthiest children in the land at some expensive private schools I have visited.)

The question of behaviour is really: what do we do when children don't follow our instructions, and don't focus on the work? And therein lies the rub.

When they don't follow the rules

There are two schools of behaviour management, broadly speaking. One school is: we need to work *with* children to persuade them to learn. The other is: we need to impose sanctions on children so they are made to learn. In general, I lean towards the latter. It is my belief that the teacher should be the authority in the classroom, and therefore a breach of that authority should meet with a sanction. When children suffer repeated and reliably enforced sanctions, they learn – sooner or later – not to do the thing you did not want them to do. No child on the planet yearns to sit in detention.

One issue I take with the first school of thought, that we work *with* children to persuade them to learn, is that it takes a lot longer to get right. This school is what I would call the 'Bill Rogers' style of behaviour management. His book, *Classroom Behaviour*, has long been a staple for new teachers. I myself found it extremely helpful as a new teacher, mainly because he includes a lot of dialogue between teacher and student, and as a new teacher you often simply *do not know what to say*, and Rogers gives you the lines.

But the issue for me is that this school of thought often emphasises aspects that sit uneasily with me: giving students 'take-up time,' which means not expecting them to follow your instructions straight away. 'De-escalation,' which means not imposing stronger sanctions when children behave worse and worse. 'Ignoring secondary behaviours,' such as rolling eyes and tutting, which I would argue are ruder than whispering and so, for that pupil to turn into a decent, polite human being, should really be met with *stronger* sanctions than the original offence.

The problem with kids is that they are kids. We can't assume they will make the right choice. Sometimes children do, and sometimes they don't. With some 'edge-case' kids, sometimes they make the right choice, but mostly they don't. Children are not fully formed beings like adults are, and some days their entire reason for being, when teenagers, is to push boundaries. That's right, adolescents are pre-programmed to see how much they can get away with, a fact of life pretty much any parent will attest to.

So I would argue we need, desperately need, sanctions which are swift and certain – and I would agree absolutely with Bill Rogers himself who says that 'it is not the severity of the consequence, but the certainty'[2] that matters. It doesn't really matter much whether your detention is 15 minutes or 50 minutes – the pupil will feel it. In fact, I would start small so you have room to escalate if you need to.

Be proactive

But before we talk about sanctions too much, there is a crucial step before that. The best behaviour management is proactive, not reactive. We as teachers need to focus on ensuring pupils don't misbehave in the first place. We need to try and get pupils to make good behaviour a habit. This means explicitly teaching children how to behave.

Even if we think pupils know how to behave, it is unlikely all their previous teachers had exactly the same expectations and rules. It is far better to be explicit up front. This also helps to quash later 'but nobody told me' complaints. A friend of mine completing her PGCE was recently charged with 'going much harder' on a class she had been too 'soft' with in terms of her behaviour management. My first piece of advice was to *narrate exactly what the new rules were and why*. Teachers can't just turn up to a lesson having apparently had a personality transplant. Kids need more lead-in time than that. In the subsequent discussion I go through exactly how to establish your expectations for this reason.

School context

Having worked in a number of different schools, it's worth making a point about school context and how much that plays into what you do in the classroom.

In a really good school, where behaviour is recognised by other teachers and external visitors (like, but not exclusively, Ofsted) to be excellent, your job as a teacher should be to enforce behaviour by following the school's policy. You should avoid being markedly less or more strict than the school's average teacher, though all teachers are on a spectrum of strictness. What children really need is consistency, and if they are normally reminded not to whisper, and that reminder is enough to ensure they don't whisper again, you will be making life very hard for yourself if you insist on slapping a detention on anyone for the same misdemeanour. It takes time to acclimatise when you move schools, but if the ambient behaviour of the children is already excellent, you can just slot into that process.

If, on the other hand, your school's behaviour is bad, then you might need to steel yourself to be the strictest teacher in a lax school. This is a hard road, and one I would advise to choose with caution, because unless your pupils like you they will absolutely push against every one of your 'unfair' sanctions and 'unfair' rules. On the other hand, if you allow pupils to misbehave in lesson after lesson, you will be completely miserable, and they will learn very little. So it's really about choosing your poison here.

Love the kids

I think it's important to address the issue of 'likeability' here. Lots of people in teaching, and people I hugely respect, will say that it doesn't matter whether the children like you, as long as they *respect* you. In some ways, this makes sense. It is clearly more important for children to respect you than to like you. And yet I think that everything becomes easier when children *do* like you. With a really tricky class in a really tricky school, it can work wonders to go in soft, win the class over, and then ramp up expectations while *taking the class with you*. You have to be on the same side as the kids. Teaching is not a battle, even though it can feel like one sometimes. You're both running for the same destination; it's more like the kids sometimes run off the beaten track and you sort of need to scoop them back onto it sometimes. The kids need to know that you like them – in fact, I'd say for our most deprived children, they actually need to know that you *love* them, because they might not hear that word as often as they should.

In my second year of teaching I taught a child who had experienced extreme trauma and whose family were in grave emotional and financial difficulties.

I imposed strict sanctions to try to get her to behave, but she continued to fight against everything I did. Her Head of Year and I sat down with the child, and that was when I first heard the 'l' word and all its magic: 'Miss isn't giving you detentions because she hates you. Miss loves you!' The girl looked at me for confirmation. The Head of Year nodded encouragingly at me. 'It's true. I do love you. I want the best for you!' The girl's behaviour didn't magically transform overnight, but it was the start of a long journey that ended with her success in public examinations, and to her generally not being awful in lessons anymore (and, truth be told, to her becoming maybe one of my all-time favourite students ever). I tried the same thing later that term with another tricky customer, and again found their attitude transforming. Since then, when any child has said, 'I hate you!' I have replied, 'well, I love you, and that's why I'm [insert literally anything I'm doing here].'

Now, don't go declaring love of all random children you teach – this will raise more than a few eyebrows. But you can definitely tell a class you love teaching them, you think they're a great team, you look forward to your lessons. And then the kids you must have lots of tricky conversations with, you can reserve the love for.

Expectations

When I was training to teach, I was perplexed to be told repeatedly: 'decide what your expectations are before you go into the classroom. If someone doesn't have a pen, what do you do?' The problem was, I didn't *know* what to do. And the problem seems to be that, if a kid doesn't have a pen, in some schools you give them a pen; in other schools you give them a detention – and there are a world of other options between those two extremes.

Let's simplify matters for new teachers. Eventually, you will come up with a multitude of possibilities for different circumstances. But, I would start with some clear ground rules. Start by telling the kids you expect two things: they follow all your instructions, because (if you feel you need to justify this to them) you are the teacher and the person who knows how best to help them succeed; and they focus 100% on the work. Anything that distracts from that focus will be met with a consequence – here is where you use your school's system (it might be a demerit, a C– point, a warning, and so on). So: a kid doesn't have a pen? That's pretty distracting for the other kids in the class, which means they can't 100% focus on their work. Consequence. A child asks 'why?' before following an instruction? That's ground rule one broken. Consequence. (Though a caveat: especially when you start at a new school – and even as a seasoned teacher – I would explain *everything* to the kids, so they never have an excuse to talk back. For example, 'turn to page 10 where we finished off yesterday. Yes, I know you weren't here, Callum, but still, you will turn to page 10 and we will sort that out later.' 'Stand outside, because you're causing a disruption that is stopping your classmates from focusing on the work.' 'Hand me the phone, because I know you are not meant to be playing with that during lessons.' 'I'm giving you a warning, because you know the expectation is that you are silent.' And so on, ad absolute infinitum.)

Let's talk more about establishing those expectations. We know broadly *what* to say – the two major classroom rules, every other rule you can think of being really a sub-rule of those two – but what about when and how to say it? The first lesson is often an administrative nightmare, with seating plans to orchestrate, books to be handed out, and registers to be taken. I would say you need to make your ground rules clear immediately following the essential admin (either they are sitting where you want them to sit, or, in some schools, they are sitting and you have taken a register).

When you address the class with these simple expectations, there is no need to put on your 'strict teacher' face. Having strict rules does not mean you are a nasty teacher. Quite the opposite. Having strict rules means you love children and want the best for them. Make sure you communicate that with your face and body language. In fact, if you consistently and calmly use sanctions and systems, there is really no need to shout at all in the classroom if you don't want to. I personally was never much of a shouter before I became a Head of Year, and it was felt that some children needed a bit of a rocket one to one. To this day, I have not shouted at a whole class. Now, I reserve the right to do so in the future, as I'm not opposed to shouting for any reason other than it hurts my voice, and I sound like a bit of an idiot when I do it. Find your teacher persona and live it. I am extremely strict, and in any school I've worked in I have become known as such, but that doesn't mean I have to raise my voice. I'm never trying to intimidate or scare children; I'm trying to make sure the classroom is as calm and happy as it can be.

When you use strict sanctions, you don't have to raise your voice. If the child shouts back, you just apply the next sanction. 'It's a shame you've been so rude, Shauna; you did have a 20-minute detention with me, but now I will have to refer you to the Head of Year's detention. I'm disappointed you're continuing to be rude, because now I will have to have you removed and in the isolation room today.' The thing this modus operandi does give you is the ability to say to children: 'I'm *never* rude to you. I don't expect you to be rude to me,' a quid pro quo all but the most intransigent students will acknowledge.

You don't need to establish your expectations every lesson, and with some classes once will be enough. But with other classes, you will want to seize the opportunity to reset them: 'Yesterday I had to give three detentions to people in this class. Three! That means three of you were really unfocused, and that stopped your classmates from learning as much as they could. Today, I want 100% focus from 100% of you. Let's make this a detention-free lesson for all of us.'

Positivity

Which leads us on to positivity. Especially in the strictest schools, positivity is massively important. As Doug Lemov writes, if we want to be really, really strict we must be really, really *really* warm.[3] The core of this is making sure you genuinely *like* children, and, in particular, you like the children in front of you. In hiring teachers, I've always said: if they like kids and they possess basic common sense, we can make them into an excellent teacher. (In a culture of recruitment crisis, this is a stance that makes sense, I think.)

When you genuinely like children, and you are excited to come and see them every day, positivity and warmth should be evident from just looking at your face. If you're someone who tends to hide your positive emotions, stop it now. The kids need to know you're happy to be there.

If teachers inject their lessons with a good dose of positivity from the outset, it sets the tone: we make the weather in our classrooms. If we come in, excited to teach, excited for the kids to learn, and knowing they can and will behave, it makes a difference. Our enthusiasm rubs off. So, before each lesson, even in the depths of dark winter mornings after a long parents' evening the night before, remember how many people go to work each day and sit at a desk and ask themselves: 'what value am I adding to the world?' You, as a teacher, never need to ask yourself that question. Yes, teaching might be one of the hardest jobs you could have chosen, but it is also one of the best: a social and moral good, combined with chatting about a subject you (presumably) love with awesome kids all day. What could be better? Keep that in mind as you narrate to the class what you'll be covering in your lesson, smiling and noticing good things.

In my first year of teaching, I was told to 'notice three good things for every bad thing'; at one school I worked at, our rule of thumb was 'three merits for every demerit.' This holds true across contexts. If you need to issue a lot of corrections, get ready to notice a lot of good things too. Notice the kid sitting up, pen in hand, eager to learn. Notice the kid who puts their hand up to answer every question, even when they get some wrong. Notice the kid whose writing is beautiful, or lengthier than you might expect. Notice the way an answer includes extra information. As you notice all of these things, say them out loud. This is something Lee Canter explains well in *Assertive Discipline*: he calls it 'narrating the positive.'[4] It's not about praise, because when you start telling kids 'well done' for holding a pen in their hands they assume you think they're a moron. It's just about saying what you see, preferably using names. Children are almost always looking for attention: make sure there is plenty of positive attention to go around, and they are far less likely to seek negative attention instead.

Soft vs. strong

Behaviour management is a tricky balance: you don't want to be too soft, and you don't want to be too strong.

If you are a softie, your classes will probably love you – at first. They will be thrilled that *finally* someone understands that it's just *no big deal* if their shirts are untucked, or if they have a bit of a chat while they do the work. The problem is, the atmosphere of a classroom where things slide can all too easily swerve to anarchy, and then almost no children are happy. Remember, if you're the softest teacher in the school, you are probably a bit of a walkover. Remember the impact your choices as the softie have on the poor teacher who gets the class after you – both the period after, and the one who inherits them after a year of indulging in their bad habits. You're not only making life harder for your future self, you're also making life harder for your colleagues.

But there are also risks of being overly strict. If you are strict – upholding every tiny rule, barking instructions, telling children off when they get something wrong – and you do none of this with love, or loving explanations, the children might behave, but they will do so from *fear* of you. Now, most people have teachers in their past who they remember as the terrifying strict teachers, and most adults will (at least grudgingly) admit that they actually learned an awful lot from those teachers. But I'm of the opinion that you don't want to be that teacher. You don't want to go into every lesson only seeing negatives. Being a teacher is partly about issuing constant reminders of your expectations of behaviour – accept that, and move on. Don't be frustrated that the kids just never seem to *remember* to take their pens out naturally at the start of a lesson. Just tell them anew each lesson, again, and again, and again, with love.

Follow the policy

The most important rule of behaviour management is to follow your school's behaviour policy. There are nuances to this that will be unwritten. For example, on paper it might state some misdemeanours deserve a consequence, but in practice teachers will firstly give warnings for these things. It is important to observe a range of teachers managing behaviour at any new school so you start to get a sense of how the behaviour policy plays out in reality. You can, of course, decide to be tougher than the other teachers in your school, but being the strictest teacher in a school that is quite lax, as I've said, is a tough road to go down (that said, if you're in it for the long haul, the payoff that is lovely, beautifully behaved classes, can be worth it).

Your school, nine times out of ten, will have some kind of behaviour policy. This will outline the sanctions you can use. If it does not, sanctions should include: detentions (five minutes and upwards; check your school's upper limit and sequence your sanctions accordingly. These are also often divided between teacher detentions, and Head of Department, Head of Year, or Leadership Team detentions depending on the severity of the offence), removal from class (hopefully not just to another room on the same corridor), negative phone call home (unreliable: remember, the kids whose behaviour is the worst are often correlated with children whose families are hard to reach), referral to a senior member of staff, and (ineffectual at best) being put 'on report' to someone. Before you get in the classroom, seek clarity on when these sanctions apply. It might be helpful to ask questions such as:

- What happens if someone forgets equipment?

- What if someone talks over me?

- What if a pupil is rude to another pupil?

- What if a pupil is rude to me?

- What happens when pupils don't follow instructions?

- Do we sanction daydreaming/not writing enough, or do we only sanction behaviour that distracts others?

Simply asking your line manager, or an experienced teacher at that school, how they would sanction the aforementioned offences should give you a fairly good idea of what you are going to be expected to do in different situations.

Public or private?

One thing to note when you look at how other teachers apply the behaviour policy is whether warnings are issued privately or publicly. I'm not a fan of warnings myself, because it feels too much like a 'free ride' for a misbehaving student, but these are normally a 'must-have' in schools' behaviour policies.

In the vast majority of schools, warnings will be a private affair. This is usually because teachers fear pupils lashing out if they are upbraided for their behaviour in front of a class, leading to even worse behaviour. To give a private warning, you simply move close to the student, and whisper: 'that's a warning. You can't call out – it disrupts the learning of the whole class,' or 'you've got a warning, because the instruction was to begin writing, but you are just staring into space.' Often, these warnings are combined with a glimpse of what might happen in the future: 'you've got a warning; it will be a detention if you continue to. . . .'

There are two major downsides to giving warnings privately. The first is that, if you are whispering, the pupil may genuinely not hear you, or they may *pretend* not to hear you. Then, when you issue a sanction, they have the excuse of being able to contest this 'unfair' decision because they 'didn't get a warning.' If this does happen, I would strengthen the sanction, because children need to learn that arguing back rudely leads to worse things happening. I would say something like: 'you did have a 20-minute detention, but it will be 30 minutes now because you have reacted so badly. It's important to learn to control your reactions.'

The second issue with giving private warnings is that *no one else hears you.* OK, perhaps the two or three students near the offender realise what you're doing, but it is entirely possible when you issue a private warning that the majority of the class thinks: 'annoying that Marcus is called out and got away with it. Perhaps I can call out and get away with it too.' Some children may think that kids in your class get away with poor behaviour; other children may imagine they *too* can likewise get away with misbehaving.

A public warning just means you are at the front, calling attention to the child who has misbehaved, rather than whispering next to them. The obvious drawbacks with this are that you then need to stop your lesson in order to issue the warning, though you need to do this with private warnings too when you are teaching. The second drawback is that this calls attention to the behaviour that has happened in your room, which may make kids who hadn't actually noticed it think: 'oh, bad behaviour is happening in this room. Maybe I can get in on the fun and behave badly too.'

I would issue public warnings as rapidly as possible to ensure the misbehaviour does not distract from the learning of the class. You can just break off midway through your sentence, saying: 'Jessica, that's a warning – all eyes on me.' This works when the children respect you, and when behaviour is already fairly good in your classroom. This also, incidentally, works when behaviour is fairly poor, because if the ambient noise level is high, it's pointless to whisper anything to anyone – after all, nobody else is.

The other use of public warnings is to warn a class anonymously. This includes saying things like: 'I'm disappointed that *some of you* think it's ok to daydream instead of focusing. It isn't. You are wasting your learning time.' Or: 'I'm waiting for 100%. . . . Thank you.' In schools with good behaviour and compliant children, using an anonymous public warning should result in the behaviour you're looking for. Some children just need to be reminded of the expectations. One teacher I know, who hated the idea of the 'warning free-ride' used to give the class a warning to begin: 'you know my expectations. This is your warning. Any misbehaviour will be met with a sanction.'

Sanctions

When issuing sanctions, you can follow the same guidelines as previously discussed for publicly or privately issuing them. You may have to write the sanction in their planner – have a look at your school's policy. Most crucially, you need to keep track of who you have given a sanction to. If a child is issued a detention and they don't turn up and *you don't notice*, it will be basically impossible to enforce better behaviour in the future – you have just handed over your only teacher power to the child.

In schools without centralised detentions, holding detentions becomes the mainstay of many teachers' lives. You need to decide when to hold your detention. Lunchtime can be a good time for you, especially if you have after-school commitments. But be careful not to hold it over the whole of lunch break – after all, children do need to eat in that time. If you school seats year groups at particular times for lunch, holding a lunchtime detention can become impractical, as the children will always be late or need to leave early. It also ties you to your classroom for the whole of the lunch break. That said, if you find yourself there anyway, you can just get children to clock in and clock out (by which I mean, you write down the time they arrive and calculate the time they say they need to leave, and make them sit any overflow minutes after school or the next day).

After-school detentions are a bit of a minefield. The worst children will definitely have more detentions than just yours to attend. If you have an online system, you can check this; if you don't, you just have to relentlessly follow up. Much of my early years of teaching were spent 'chasing detentions.' Often, children will simply not attend after school. You then need to find the child the next day to inform them that their detention has doubled, or whatever the next step in the school's behaviour policy is. Beware of escalations that involve other people: if your Head of Year doesn't bother to hold detentions as per the policy, you will undermine yourself by following it. You must insist the detention time is served, or behaviour in your classroom will never improve. Occasionally, you will need to call parents to let them know when a consequence is missed.

On your own?

If it's down to you and you alone to set behaviour expectations and sanctions, keep it simple. I would give one warning, and then a sanction. Before giving a child a named warning, make sure you are constantly reinforcing your expectations anonymously, but picking up on children who aren't following them. Make your sanctions short, but certain. Relentlessly follow up to ensure all children attend your detentions – it might take a year, or even two – but it is worth the investment; eventually they will realise that you mean what you say and it is pointless to fight it. Escalate to your line manager using the school system, but if there isn't one, call parents and try to get them on board.

I don't believe there is anything more needlessly time consuming in schools than chasing up missed detentions. The amount of teacher time being spent in schools all across the country on this kind of administration is inconceivably huge. An increasing number of schools are instituting centralised detentions. I think this is an immensely good thing, which I go into in a subsequent section I would love school leaders to take special heed of.

Parents

A word about parents first though. They will generally fall into one of three camps: supportive, unsupportive, and unavailable. Thankfully, you will probably find most parents extremely supportive. That does not immediately translate to being effective. As a pastoral school leader, I was always shocked by the number of times a child would be defiant to their parent in a meeting about behaviour, and how the parent would just say, 'that's just how he is,' with a sigh and a wry smile. That isn't just how he is: all children have the potential to be good, decent, and polite members of society. We just need to hold them to that standard constantly. It's hard for parents, and it's hard for teachers.

When talking to parents about behaviour, the crucial point to bear in mind is that they love their child more than you can possibly imagine (unless you are a parent yourself; then you will know). That love does not always translate to doing what is in their child's best interest, but it is there. Try and find some common ground on this love first.

It is best to deal with parents pre-emptively. If you are inheriting a class, find out who the troublemakers are. Focus your early lessons on ensuring these children succeed, and pre-emptively call their parents to tell them of their successes, or even just that they have impressed you in these first lessons. In many cases, this will be the first positive phone call they have had about their child. This will be invaluable to refer back to if (or when. . .) their child has done something less impressive in the future. The parent will remember you as someone who really championed their child from the start.

In any phone conversation, I would avoid speaking in purely negative terms about the child in question. Remember always that no child is 'horrible.' They're just a child, and they're trying to figure out their way in the world, and sometimes they do horrible things. But the magical thing about dealing with children all day is that there is, in every child, no matter how difficult, a wonderful human being waiting to be drawn out. I would always begin a conversation by telling a parent you know the child has great potential – after all, this isn't a lie; all children have great potential. Include some specific things the child has done really well. Then explain the child's behaviour, and let their parent respond.

Often, parents will start to make excuses here. Many of our most troubled children come from troubled homes, and these excuses won't be lies. But you need to try and get parents away from focusing on what they can't control. At the same time, they're human beings, and empathy goes a long way. Just listening to a parent's woes and sympathising with them will often help to get them on your side.

I would then give parents advice on how to support the school. Saying something like: 'this is Emily's fourth detention in two weeks. I'm not sure it's working. Perhaps you could take away phone privileges, or something she really likes, each time she gets a detention? Then she knows we're a team working together to help her to behave and focus in lessons.' If you have time, ask the parent what their child really loves to do, and work out a way that they can use incentives outside school along with sanctions to support their child's behaviour in school.

Similar rules apply when meeting parents in person. If you're a new teacher, you shouldn't be expected to have parent meetings (apart from, obviously, parents' evenings) without your Head of Department or Head of Year present, so do ask them for this support (though you might not get it). Again, start by saying what the child is doing well, and try to get in the idea that you like their child. Remember, the parent's only knowledge of you is filtered by a child you've been disciplining, and they need to be reassured that you genuinely love their child and want the best for them.

Explain the child's behaviour, but always avoid attributing any of their actions to their character: the focus is that, while the child behaves poorly, they are intrinsically a good person. Ask the parent what their child is like at home – this will often give you a good insight. If the parent is struggling with their child's behaviour (and I would say this is the case in at least 50% of parent meetings I've held), share some tips and suggestions.

Don't expect parents to solve everything. Plenty will be supportive of the school in general, but far too busy with their own lives to do much more than say they support the school. Some parents will be absolute gems – when a year 11 stormed out of my after-school revision class and refused to attend, I called her parent straight away, who was livid. Literally five minutes passed, and the child returned to my classroom, saying, 'my Mum says to apologise and promise to attend every revision class.' I started to tell her off as her phone began to buzz repeatedly, and she said, frustrated, 'It's my Mum. . . .' She showed me her screen, which consisted of her mother sending message after message reading: 'are you there? Have you said sorry? ARE YOU IN THE CLASSROOM?' (At Christmas time, this girl brought me a huge box of chocolates, and before I could thank her said, 'They're from my mum, NOT me.' She was predicted a D. She achieved a B. *That's* the difference a great parent can make.)

Other parents will be unhelpful. Some won't be able to control their own children, some will have phones which are never answered, some will have had a terrible experience of education themselves and be openly hostile to you and the school. In these situations, note it, and don't waste your time calling in future. Some parents will desperately want to support you, but simply won't have the language skills to be able to communicate effectively, perhaps because they are new to the country. In time, this can change. But it is undeniable that some children become the whole responsibility of the school community to raise. It might not seem right, but we have a responsibility to do it if no one else will.

Tough conversations

While sanctions are a crucial cornerstone to our schools, what is most important is the accompanying conversation around the sanction. We need to be prepared to have tough conversations with children to help them to change their behaviour in the future.

If you are having a tough conversation with a pupil, a few guidelines might help. Ensure it really is a tough conversation. I've been guilty in the past of being too pally with kids, or shaking detention off as 'only 20 minutes.' Pupils need to see detention as something really serious that most people aren't in – ensure you reinforce this. ('Where are your friends right now? Yes – at home, not in this room.') Try and get them to take responsibility for their actions. Plenty of adults find this hard, and you can bet children find this even harder. But if you can start to get children to realise that it is *their actions* that have consequences, and that they alone have the power to change those actions, you might be onto a winner for a long-term responsible mindset. Try and connect the child's behaviour to their future success – if they continue to behave like this, their future will not be as bright. Mention what happens when you disagree with your boss, perhaps, and how you handle that (hopefully it is not by storming out of the room shouting). Finally, never lose the opportunity to reinforce the fact that giving sanctions is actually the *caring* thing to do. You might even point out that it is far easier for teachers not to bother giving sanctions at all – they just want to teach their subject without having to stop and talk about behaviour. But teachers give sanctions because they *love* their pupils, and desperately want them to learn what is the right way to behave.

For leaders

The next section mainly applies to those who have the power to change a school's systems – if that's not you, it will be soon. Read it anyway.

Centralised detentions

A centralised detention means having one big detention hall that everyone's detainees go to for their detention at the end of the school day. It can be run by two, or even one, strong member/s of staff as needed. It can be run on a rota, so one person isn't staying an hour after school each day, as many teachers will be doing in their individual classes. Because the children all end up in the same place, there is no issue of 'clashes,' because if a child has accrued two detentions from two different teachers, they simply serve these detentions one after the other. At one school I worked at, we had four 20-minute slots after school and one 20-minute slot at lunch. On the very rare occasion a pupil accrued more than five detentions in a day, the child would go to isolation. This was partly so they could not be in circulation, as they were clearly having too bad a day to be in lessons, and partly because we really believed it was important for children to endure their sanctions on the day they were given. We did not believe in rolling over detentions to the following day; too many children forget what they are in detention for, and that is how resentment against a school grows.

With a centralised detention, the teacher's only administration is to log it on a centralised system. This can have its issues – people forgetting to log detentions can really undermine the system, and senior leaders in these systems will need to be relentless about pushing the message to ensure everyone logs their detentions. Because administration is reduced, teachers tend to consistently use the system.

In other schools where I have worked, some teachers would apply the behaviour system as it was intended to be applied, but other teachers would stop bothering. It's a hard job, and even teachers with the best will in the world will decide something has to give. If it's the 20 minutes they don't have to chase up a 20-minute detention given and missed yesterday when they could be planning or organising feedback for their pupils, that doesn't sound like too mad a trade-off, until you take into account the impact on the whole school of some teachers setting behaviour standards and other teachers letting them slide.

One powerful argument against centralised detentions is that children need to connect the teacher with the sanction. I can assure you, pupils in a centralised system are *very* aware of who has given them the detention. This kind of information is imprinted at the moment of the detention being issued. But they don't always know *why* they are in that detention. One school I know of insists that teachers come down to the detention hall to speak with their detainees during the detention slot, which I think works nicely, but is difficult to keep track of. This would be something your school would need to think carefully about staffing and pushing prior to being introduced.

Another option is to have a point person, such as a Head of Year or Head of Department, responsible for having conversations with *all* the children in their year group or subject department in the detention hall. The conversation is often remarkably similar: adult asks child, 'Why are you in detention?' Child says: 'I don't know. I didn't do anything!' Adult probes deeper, child describes what happened. Adult explains how this behaviour is unacceptable and asks the child to rethink how to behave next time. Having one person deliver the message has the added benefit of consistency of message: these restorative conversations are some of the toughest things in behaviour management to get right, and they're not something we're all trained in.

Setting school policy

If you're in the lucky position of being able to set a whole-school behaviour policy, I think you need to make it as simple as possible. I would have three steps to it, and no more. The first step should be a behaviour point – whether that is a C point, demerit, or something else – that, while being logged on a system, is not linked to a sanction. The child knows their behaviour is unacceptable, and there was no warning (though in effect, as this is not linked to a sanction, you can think of this as a warning if you wish) but they knew straight away their behaviour was not acceptable.

At the second offence, give them a second behaviour point that *is* linked to a sanction. Usually that will be a detention. Make that detention longer than ten minutes, but it doesn't have to be radically long or it will become hard to staff if the child accrues too many.

At the third offence, the child is showing they are unable to learn from the sanctions being given. Have them removed from the teacher's room at this point.

The removal should be something worse than being in the lesson, or there should be an expectation of a certain amount of work done, or you will find children with the weakest motivation actually choosing to be removed after a detention has been issued.

Have some go-to straight detentions, by all means, but try and make these easy to remember. Lack of equipment, for example, should be a detention, but ensure only the form tutor gives this, so no teacher has to later log a detention for essentially the same thing. If a child is late to school, this should probably be a straight detention, but you can have someone in your school office log these. If a child has done no homework at all, this should probably be a straight detention – class teachers will need to log these.

In terms of what system you use, make it easy for teachers to log. Don't have thousands of codes they need to put in. One school I worked at had its first behaviour point as a specific thing, so for each and every child you had to log: C1 – late to lesson, or C1 – talking, or C1 – disrupting, or C1 – interrupting. This is unnecessarily cumbersome. Instead, ensure teachers can pull up a class list, and have a button to click next to each child to denote the level of sanction – C1 – demerit/warning, C2 – detention, C3 – removal. At one school I worked at, we asked teachers to leave the comment box blank if the issue was behaviour, so Heads of Year always knew no comment meant poor behaviour. If the child had been removed from the teacher's lesson, we asked the teacher to put a brief comment in so the form tutor and Head of Year could understand what was happening for that to occur.

Of course, one tricky aspect of behaviour management we won't cover here is how leaders ensure the system is being used consistently by all teachers. In brief, ensure someone is responsible for this, ensure they are on the ground looking at classrooms every day, and ensure they have frequent opportunities to provide feedback on behaviour to the whole staff.

Schools should never stop making behaviour a priority. It is dangerous to ever feel like you have 'cracked' behaviour as a school. I'm not sure any school ever will. Children will push limits, and while whole-school behaviour can improve dramatically over time, it will always be something school leaders need to repeatedly and frequently check in on.

Once you have decent behaviour, though, you can start thinking about the best way to teach. Before you think about how to teach, though, it is clear you need to first know what to teach – which is the subject of the next chapter.

Put simply

- Instead of worrying about oppressing children with your rules, remember you are teaching polite habits.

- Instead of doling out sanctions, start small so you can escalate and explain everything.

- Instead of devising a system, follow the policy.

Notes

1 Will Durant, *The Story of Philosophy*, p. 98 (Pocket Books, 1991).
2 Bill Rogers, *Classroom Behaviour*, p. 9 (Sage Publications Ltd., 2006).
3 Doug Lemov, *Teach Like a Champion 2.0*, p. 438 (Jossey Bass, 2015).
4 Lee Canter, *Assertive Discipline* (Solution Tree, 2009).

3   **What to teach**

The question of what to teach in schools is surprising in its controversy. The problem of what to teach is perhaps inevitably coupled with the question: what is the purpose of school? Your answer to this question will usually colour your opinion of what to teach.

What is the purpose of schools?

If you believe the purpose of schools is to ensure pupils achieve great results, then you will want to teach children how to pass tests extremely well.

If you believe that the purpose of schools is to ensure pupils are well-rounded, happy individuals, then you may well teach 'soft skills' and prioritise character education, along with investing in extra-curricular activities.

If you believe the purpose of schools is to ensure pupils' lives are changed by what they learn, you will probably prioritise a curriculum that thinks about enduring ideas rather than what is fashionable, or what is on current exam papers.

If you believe that the purpose of schools is to prepare children for the world beyond school, you will want them to have work experience and, again, the soft skills needed in employment.

The reality is that most schools believe a combination of these aspects.

For my two pence, I think that the purpose of schools is to broaden pupils' horizons, both literally and less tangibly. Literally: children should get better results than they would have done had they not attended the school, opening more doors to them in the future. Intangibly: for the rest of their lives, those who have attended the school should have an enriched experience because of what they learned at school.

Who chooses?

But who chooses the curriculum? Matthew Arnold might have advocated teaching 'the best that has been thought and said,' but for generations educationalists have interrogated: 'according to who?'

Who decides what is the best? Any curriculum maker's job is fraught with the political. Take English. If you prioritise the most enduring works, or 'the canon,' you would be forgiven for feeling uneasy at its lack of representativeness. Most writers in the traditional canon are Western, white males. Is that really 'the best'?

Some argue that, more important than 'best' is 'most influential.' Maya Angelou has written than she first imagined Shakespeare as 'a black woman' because his works were so easy to relate to.[1] It is impossible, moreover, to read Jean Rhys's *Wide Sargasso Sea*, a more modern text, without knowledge of Charlotte Brontë's *Jane Eyre*, the text Rhys's is based on. Some literary theorists argue that all literature is 'intertextual,' that every text is linked to every other text, and so really we should work out what the 'cornerstone' pieces are and ensure all teachers teach those.[2]

English is just one subject area, and you can already see that curriculum choice is full of difficulties.

In general, though, a good principle of choosing what goes into a curriculum is the stuff without which the other stuff cannot be understood. In maths, for example, it is really hard to understand trigonometry or algebra if you can't understand the basics of number bonds or times tables. If your concept of number is underdeveloped, the more refined aspects of the subject will always be a mystery to you.

Prior attainment

The other difficulty with what to teach is that some children arrive at secondary school very far behind their peers. It is all well and good to point to Eton and say 'if they can study Dostoyevsky, so can our children,' but if your pupils are struggling to read polysyllabic words, it can be argued that to push the most difficult literature into their curriculum actually does them a disservice.

Which raises the uncomfortable question: do different children require different curricula? If that is the case, won't the middle-class children, who arrive so far ahead of their peers anyway, be granted yet *another* way to be further ahead than their less advantaged peers?

The brutal reality is that teachers of disadvantaged pupils need to do more in less time. They need to move children to an end point that is far more distant when setting off than it is for the more advantaged children, and they need to do it while navigating a political minefield that private schools are largely exempt from.

The moral conundrum

The difficulty is, as I'm often reminded by teacher friends, that we have a duty to teach children right and wrong. It is clearly an historical injustice that our canon of English literature is overwhelmingly white. Yet, to teach less enduring texts simply to tick the 'colour box' is also reductive to that literature's impact on our society. One of my past colleagues, an English teacher from Ghana, told me that her education in literature was 'overwhelmingly white,' but when she attended university she became fascinated by African literature. When I asked if she regretted not having studied this in school, she replied that she did not – school had given her the 'grounding' in the classics to ensure she could read widely and understand all areas of literature, along with, importantly, instilling a love of reading, which meant that she could read into her area of choice at university level. There is a powerful argument made in some areas of education that we ought to redress this omission much earlier in a child's education.

Skills curriculum

Perhaps in part to avoid such difficult questions as to what we choose to teach, teachers prior to 2010 had been encouraged to consider teaching the 'skills' of their subject, rather than the content being taught. In this way, you could teach generic skills through any content. If you taught history, you would teach the skill of source analysis, and it didn't much matter if you were exploring Nazi Germany or the transatlantic slave trade, because the crucial thing was the skill itself.

If you look at the government's national curricula prior to 2010, you will see a massive focus on skills – reading skills, analysis skills, numeracy skills. These documents discuss the skills at length, with almost no mention of the content.

We see the legacy of this skills agenda in the current English GCSEs, with rubrics which are composed of skills with only 'indicative content' to guide examiners, always included with the proviso that candidates do not *need* to include *any* of this content to be awarded marks. In English Language GCSE, there is still no specified *content* knowledge to be taught *at all*.

Why is this a problem? Surely skills is democratising – surely this means that pupils are on a fair playing field, and children who have read more are therefore not advantaged?

The knowledge issue

The difficulty is that there is a huge knowledge component to reading. E.D. Hirsch encapsulates this most clearly when he writes: 'reading comprehension is *not* a general skill that can be developed . . . to enhance comprehension abilities there needs to be systematic knowledge building with more whole-class instruction and discussion. . . . The actual difficulty of a book is highly dependent on an individual student's familiarity with the topic.'[3] He cites the 1998 Recht-Leslie study which shows that '"poor readers" outperformed "good readers" when the poor readers knew more about the subject matter – in this case, baseball. . . . The meaning of a text is constructed from both presented information and reader-contributed information.' He goes on to cite two more studies which equally revealed that *knowledge* of the text's content led to students appearing to read much more fluently.

The more a pupil has read, the more knowledge they have, and therefore the higher the level of text they can access. Prior knowledge is indicative of reading comprehension, as evinced by the primary school children Hirsch spoke about in 2015 about who read two texts of the same 'reading age,' one about toothpaste and one about tree frogs. The children understood and could answer questions on the former, but not the latter. Why? Because they know what toothpaste is. But they've never heard of tree frogs, and so the passage was completely impenetrable to them.[4] My favourite example of this comes from Hirsch's *The Knowledge Deficit*: 'Jones sacrificed and knocked in a run.'[5] I know what every single word in that sentence means. But I have no idea what that *sentence* means. I cannot make sense of it – I cannot discern any *meaning*. This is because I have no prior knowledge of baseball. If I did have content knowledge, then I would be able to understand the sentence relates to that particular game.

So, a 'skills-based' assessment system is untenable, partly because knowledge matters. We just don't always realise that it is lack of knowledge – too often, we see 'poor reading comprehension.' But a 'skills-based' system is untenable mainly because you can't teach skills. Daisy Christodoulou puts this most eloquently in *Seven Myths about Education* when she writes: 'time spent imagining how to design a role play about complex moral issues in science is time not spent actually learning about atoms, compounds, mixtures and the state of matter. Time spent drawing pictures of beehives buzzing with idea-bees is time not spent learning important historical facts that allow pupils to create a chronological schema. Time spent on activities that are supposed to promote transferable skills is time not spent learning knowledge that will actually build transferable skills. . . . The aim of teaching transferable skills is for pupils to develop effective, all-purpose skills. But the methods used by the advocates of transferable skills ensure that their pupils will not develop such skills. That is because these methods systematically misrepresent the very nature of skills and their knowledge-bound character.'[6]

We can't teach a skill, because it's impossible to produce skilled performance independent of knowledge input. When we read excellent writing, we can't just say 'they are just really good at analysis.' No. They are displaying a huge amount of *knowledge*: knowledge of the text, quotation, technique, context; probably in addition to a knowledge of grammar and punctuation. All of those aspects of knowledge are combined together to create a 'skilled' piece of writing.

This is powerful for teachers too, because it makes our jobs so much simpler. How do you teach 'analysis'? It is basically impossible. But teaching the underpinning *knowledge* that goes into that analytical output is far, far easier. We can decide the key quotations to get the children to learn. We can teach the most important techniques to get them to write about. We can teach them the plot and characters of a novel or play so they write accurately about it. We can teach them the context of that text, and how it links to the quotations chosen. We can teach them the rudiments of grammar and sentence structure. Teaching knowledge *empowers* teachers.

We need, perhaps, to stop thinking about 'analysis,' 'inference,' and so on as 'skills,' and rather start to think of them as the output of whatever knowledge has gone in previously. Only then can we begin to create a curriculum that is easily taught, learned and tested.

Curriculum change

Of late, there has been a great deal of curriculum change in England, partially brought about by this new understanding of what we need to teach. There have been some controversial aspects of this. Nonetheless, when the government mandated that children learn two Shakespeare plays at key stage 3, most English teachers shrugged, knowing they taught three in three years and always had. More controversial was a focus in history on *English* history, which some critics felt evoked a certain uncomfortable jingoism.[7] The teaching of grammar returned, which met with outcry, in particular surrounding the more arcane terms.[8]

At GCSE level, exam boards have been tasked with 'strengthening' their assessment, which included a shift to explicitly *English* literature and away from American (again, uncomfortable response from many English teachers, academics and other interested parties),[9] and towards more unseen exams which prevented the level of preparation students had heretofore been able to carry out. The government was keen to prevent 'gaming' of subjects, and so schools entering children 'early' for GCSEs (which is code for: get them to sit the exam until they get the grade we want) were out, as now only the first sitting of a GCSE counts in a school's league tables. (If this had been the right thing for the children, we might not have seen quite such a drop.) In English, the 20% of the GCSE that was 'speaking and listening,' which in practice was teacher-assessed and basically unmoderated, was removed.

At A-level, as well, standards were raised across subjects, and children were, in general, expected to know more stuff and do tougher things. This had a huge knock-on for some subjects like maths, where children beginning the new A-level were so far below the expected level that they had to put teaching of the new specification back a year to enable teachers to better prepare pupils for the expected standard.[10] A modular approach, with AS and A level modules which pupils could retake in either year, was out, and terminal exams were back in.

All of these changes affect teachers of all year groups. The exams were strengthened to hold us and to hold pupils to a higher standard. We need to teach more stuff than ever before, and we need to work out the best way to do that. At the same time, holding children to a higher standard and expecting them to know more things can only be a good thing for them, in terms of the worlds opened up to children by a broader cultural knowledge of the intellectual world we live in.

So, how are we as educators to tackle this brave new world of learning harder stuff? We obviously need to work out what to teach children so they have the requisite knowledge to tackle these new, tougher exams.

But we're in a great place. We know how children learn, we know what they need to know to succeed at GCSE and A-level, and we know that we can break that knowledge down into smaller chunks. If we lead with knowledge in our curriculum, then the skills will develop. Yes, we need to get children to effectively practise – and more on that in a later chapter. But once we have identified the knowledge we will teach, we've covered a good chunk of designing the curriculum.

Relevance

One issue noted in the previous discussion is how to decide what to include in a school's curriculum. We can tie ourselves up in knots trying to make the curriculum 'relevant' to our students. We worry, if we are middle-class adults, about imposing our idea of what is 'best' on children who are not middle class. We worry, if we are white, about imposing what we think is 'most important' to know on those who are not white.

I don't think we are wrong to worry. I think we should be very worried indeed that the canon is so very white, male, and middle class. But I also don't think it is the place of secondary educators to challenge that. For our children to succeed in university, they will need to know that canon. Who changes what is considered the 'most important'? University professors. In the same way, social injustice is a terrible ill. But it's not our job to be warriors against social injustice through our classes. Who changes society? Politicians. It's our job to ensure our pupils make it to university, become politicians – they are the ones to change the status quo. Not us. Our job, our duty, is to enable others to change the status quo.

If we force our cultural concerns on our charges and deny them traditional knowledge, then we run the risk of stymying their success. If we send children to university interviews who don't know what their middle-class counterparts know, then they will merely feel embarrassed, not empowered. Like the politician who sends her child to the local failing comprehensive instead of an expensive private school, it might feel more 'morally right,' but it's certainly not the best choice for that individual child. (Luckily, the child of a well-educated politician will probably do fine no matter what school they attend. Unlike those born in poverty who have far less choice about what school they go to.) Yes, it might be 'more moral' to teach children lesser-known ideas that have been side-lined in our culture for decades. We might feel good about ourselves for having done that. But our children won't be empowered to change the status quo through this; in fact, they may be *barred* from accessing the route to changing things because they don't know the 'right' things.

I asked Christine Counsell, author, independent consultant, and trainer; formerly, teacher trainer (University of Cambridge) and MAT Director of Education (Inspiration Trust), how she thinks about curriculum.

1. How do you choose what to teach children?

I find the formulation, 'the best that has been thought and said' much too simplistic. I get the sentiment, but there is too much subjectivity and cultural contingency around it. I prefer the following principles:

They need to be taught subjects that derive from traditional disciplines (science, history, maths) and artistic/performance practices (music, art, literature). This is important because they need to be introduced to traditions of knowledge production and scholarly/artistic scrutiny so that they acquire powerful languages with which to communicate, think with precision, create and act. Artistic innovation, historical argument, scientific questioning . . . each of these is rendered so much more achievable if one is steeped in what has gone before. If we want to fulfil the democratic and emancipatory potential of schooling, we must have a curriculum that brings pupils into the formal academic and artistic conversations that have already taken place. Once able to recognise, comprehend, recall and use the grammar of a subject they can move about within that knowledge and increase their chances of being able to think critically, clearly and creatively. Above all, being inducted into these traditions is important because knowledge is produced and communicated socially. Pupils can't do science or art in isolation. To teach a subject is to introduce pupils to a community and its world, and gradually to fulfil the glorious promise that they, too, can be part of that community and its practices, if they so wish. This is the difference between Michael Young's stultifying 'Future 1' (learning a fixed canon in order to leave it fixed) and his 'Future 3' (learning a canon in order to understand how it came about, how it changes and how to take part in its continuing change).

Within each subject, there is a labyrinth of possibilities. So what guides the choice of the subject leader and/or senior curriculum leader (the two need to work together)? The following considerations are important, although some are more important in some subjects than others:

▪ What proportions, balances, and blends of substantive and disciplinary knowledge are necessary for pupils to enter into the conversation of this subject community sufficient to be able to participate, on leaving school, as an educated person?

▪ Where the subject – or a strand of the subject – is cumulative rather than hierarchical in its structure (e.g. history, art history, literature – where a vast range of possibilities are interchangeable) and where difficult choices have to be made, the question is, how well does this selection of substantive items become generative in showing pupils future possibilities beyond what is taught? How far does this selection act as a gateway? How far does this selection act as a broad and useful set of reference points which will enable pupils to access demanding traditions/genres/debates beyond what the school curriculum can cover? All this requires the teacher and the school to be communicating, always, the fact that 'the curriculum I teach you is not all there is; it is a threshold.'

This takes us back to the 'disciplinary' (How do professionals argue in this subject? Under what conditions can valid claims be made in this subject? What is admissible as evidence in this subject? How does judgement occur in this subject?). If the 'disciplinary' dimension is well taught, and well blended with the substantive, then the problem of content choice becomes easier. There is a realisation that a curriculum cannot be exhaustive and also that there can be no perfect choice and blend of content. Rather, the curriculum itself teaches pupils its own limitations.

2. How do you break down the knowledge that children must learn?

Secure, sophisticated accomplishment in a subject is always a composite of smaller components. These composites might take the form of a final performance: essay, musical composition, artistic performance, mathematical reasoning – or simply the accomplishment of understanding the subject itself and being able to 'read' it (being able to read historical scholarship, interpret a scientific paper, listen to and enjoy a complex and challenging piece of classical music). These composites are only attainable after the slow, painstaking graft of mastering the smaller components that sit underneath them.

In some subjects, we have research to show what might be best or better ways of moving through these through a route and at a rate that will secure sufficient fluency to progress onto more composite performance. In other subjects, it is a good deal more complex – research or experience might suggest differing or equally effective routes and rates: one might need to build into the curriculum the opportunity for the teacher to exercise judgement – that is, just how many stories of empire and emperors are necessary for pupils to have an adequately flexible grasp of the concept of empire to be able to notice it as a phenomenon or critique a commentary on it? Also, in some subjects, if you just do the components (only practicing scales, only listening to intervals, only learning small sections of a piece of music, only learning chronologies of factual events . . . and not listening to full works of music, enjoying the richness of learning a complex song or poem or soaking up a challenging argument or puzzling story in history), then one allows curricular progression to distort the intellectual life of the subject itself and one gives the child an emasculated version of the subject in which a concern for sequencing has distorted the proper experience of the subject. The best way I can sum this up is to say that the curriculum designer must constantly ask, at each stage in a curriculum:

■ Is this the moment to isolate?

■ Or is it the moment to integrate?

That is all one is doing as one looks in detail at content – either we are breaking down or we are building up. The subject itself – both its integrity as an intellectual or artistic practice and its paths of epistemic ascent – will determine the choice.

Here's what I propose. Teach children the stuff they need to know to do well in intellectual circles. And also teach them to love learning. Because if they love learning, and they know the baseline of knowledge, their inquiring minds will let them see what is beyond that. Do you think a child who is not white will never at any point say to themselves: 'I wonder what happened to people who look like me? I'd like to find out more about that'? Empowered with knowledge, and enamoured of finding out more, children of all backgrounds can achieve to the very highest levels and change the world.

Now we've decided what we're teaching, we can go about teaching it. Firstly, though, you need to concretise your 'what': what are the resources you will use to teach your curriculum?

Put simply

- Instead of choosing at random, work out what opens doors to the next bit they need to learn.

- Instead of teaching the GCSE at key stage 3, work out what prior knowledge they need to gain during KS3 to succeed in those exams.

- Instead of worrying about representativeness, choose what will propel children farthest.

Notes

1 www.diacronia.ro/ro/indexing/details/A186/pdf Accessed 16.9.18
2 www.english.cam.ac.uk/cambridgeauthors/byatt-intertextuality/ Accessed 16.9.18
3 E.D. Hirsch, *Why Knowledge Matters*, pp. 73–75 (Harvard Education Press, 2016).
4 Recording available at: https://policyexchange.org.uk/event/the-annual-education-lecture-with-e-d-hirsch/
5 E.D. Hirsch, *The Knowledge Deficit*, p. 68 (Mariner Books, 2007).
6 Daisy Christodoulou, *Seven Myths about Education*, pp. 81 and 84.
7 The *Guardian* reported on 16 February 2013 that the new curriculum was 'Overly Anglo-centric, highly prescriptive and quite dull is the thrust of their judgment. It fails, they say, to recognise that learning about the past of other cultures away from our shores is "as vital as knowledge of foreign languages to enable British citizens to understand the full variety and diversity of human life." Children will be deprived of knowledge of the "vast bulk" of the precious past by its narrow horizons, they say.' This led to a revision of the proposed content of the new history curriculum.
8 Again, the *Guardian* reported the views of a number of interested parties on 9 May 2017: 'David Crystal, one of Britain's foremost English language academics, has argued that the Spag test, and the view of language lying behind it, "turns the clock back half a century." There is too much emphasis on linguistic labelling as an end in itself, he says, rather than on using this as the starting point in discussions of effective writing. Michael Rosen, the children's author and *Education Guardian* columnist, has said we are suffering from "terminology-itis": a mistaken belief that talking about grammatical structures will improve pupils' writing. It's a waste of children's time, he says.'

9 Once more, the *Guardian* depressingly reported: 'Bethan Marshall, a senior lecturer in English at King's College London and chair of the National Association for the Teaching of English, said the list could put children off continuing English literature to A-level. She said: "Many teenagers will think that being made to read Dickens aged 16 is just tedious. This will just grind children down"' (25 May 2014).

10 On 1 December 2014 the TES reported: 'The decision to put back first teaching of the [maths] courses until September 2017 follows worries that the previous 2016 date would have left the first batch of pupils under-prepared for the new qualifications. . . . In February it was decided to delay the introduction of a new geography A-level from 2015 to 2016 for similar reason.'

4 Resources

Ask teachers what they spend the bulk of their time doing, and the answer is always: 'planning and marking.' Well, we'll talk about marking in Chapter 11. Planning is the subject of this one. In many schools, planning a lesson is focused chiefly on creating resources. For so many teachers, in my experience, there is nothing available centrally, and no single textbook which encapsulates everything they need in a lesson. Instead, teachers end up writing every aspect of the lesson they will deliver to the children. As such, 'planning' is less about how to get children to understand the learning, and more about creating the stuff to be learned.

The status quo

The traditional look for resources in a lesson is as follows. Teachers will have something subject-specific for the children to read – either a part of a textbook (perhaps photocopied), a novel found in the subject's store cupboard, or, in the least time-efficient case, a worksheet they have painstakingly crafted themselves. This will be supplemented with exercises – often on a different worksheet. They may also use example work – perhaps photocopied from another child's book, perhaps sourced from the exam website, perhaps written by the teacher. The whole enterprise is dictated by a PowerPoint of between four and 27 slides (no joke – in my third year of teaching I did have a 27-slide PowerPoint for a single 50-minute lesson). Perhaps prior to making all of these things, teachers have also written an outline of what they'd like the children to learn – what the focus of the lesson should be, and so on.

Obviously, this is a huge amount of work. When I talk to friends currently doing their PGCE, they tell me they are spending up to four hours to plan just a single lesson. When they speed up, as newly qualified teachers, it can still take between 30 minutes and an hour to plan every lesson. (Some activities, like the infamous 'card sort,' take significantly longer to plan than they do to be actually used by the children in the lesson.) If a full-time teacher is teaching 22 lessons a week, then there needs to be a quicker way to plan. Often, teachers will roll out lessons from previous years with some adaptations to save time. I'm not saying that teachers aren't strongly considering what they're doing as they plan, but the constraints of time mean we can never quite make the perfect lesson, which is what every perfectionist teacher desires.

And all of this, I would suggest, is the wrong focus. We focus far too much on *what* our children are learning during planning, and not enough on *how* we will ensure they have learned it.

Why simplify?

I think we need to radically simplify the resources we use in our lessons. Teachers are simply expected to do too much work in too little time. The result is that teachers are leaving the profession in droves, and recruitment is becoming ever more challenging. In my first year as a Head of Department, I will always remember a colleague saying, 'I won't be in teaching forever – I want to have children.' This profession, with its long holidays which should be perfect for family time, is now one that is widely seen as incompatible with what is quite a normal balance of work and life.

So, how can we reduce workload? I often say that part of leadership is getting good people to stop doing good things. Teachers will go above and beyond for their children, even at the risk of their health. Who hasn't seen a teacher work themselves into the ground, and drag themselves into school even when at death's door, because 'they couldn't bear to leave year 11 with a cover teacher'? Instead, we have to stop over-work at its source, and one of those major sources is planning.

PowerPoint

Before training as a teacher, I'm genuinely not even sure I was aware of the existence of PowerPoint. I'd certainly never used it, nor was it even installed on my computer. I'd never encountered it as a pupil in school or a student in university (although I do recall images being used in lectures, which could well have been delivered through a PowerPoint format).

It was in my second week of teacher training, in what is called a 'Second School Experience,' when I first was made aware of the programme. Preparing to teach a lesson for the first time, I met with the class's usual teacher whose opening words were: 'here's my log-in so you can make a PowerPoint. Obviously you'll want to make a PowerPoint.' It didn't seem too obvious to me then. I spent an hour or so painfully working out how to use the programme, painstakingly copying and pasting images I found at random using clipart (I hadn't yet understood how to get images from the internet onto a slide), and changing the fonts at whim. During the lesson, which was obviously a disaster for far wider-ranging reasons than the existence of PowerPoint, I remember finding the slides a hindrance rather than a help, as I awkwardly pointed to a slide from time to time, only really to justify the time that had been poured into making it.

I have been known to sweepingly declare that if schools would only ban PowerPoint, everything would get better – lessons, learning, workload. Now, I'm not knocking the intrinsic benefits of PowerPoint: it's great to display pictures to children, which can often bring a subject to life. It's also great to save paper – type your questions on it instead of on paper and you've also saved on your photocopying budget. And, for many teachers, PowerPoint is described as a 'crutch' to help them to deliver a coherent lesson. All of these things are true.

But I do think there are some very real drawbacks of PowerPoint we need to be aware of. Using PowerPoint inevitably leads to life in a dark room. To ensure all pupils can see the PowerPoint, you need to close the blinds. The first time I visited a school, after six interim years of work and study, my first thought was how dark it was. It was the end of the academic year and so bright and beautiful outside, but in classroom after classroom it was beyond winter. It was hellishly dark, and with the blinds drawn and no air circulating the classrooms were sweltering. I wondered how the kids could even see what they were writing in their exercise books, as the only light was the faint screen's glimmer, which barely reached beyond the front row. Much like modern family life, everyone seemed orientated towards the bright screen at the front. It was depressing.

Secondly, PowerPoint splits kids' focus. You want them to focus on you and your instruction – but instead, they are focused on the screen that bears the remnants of that instruction. You want them to focus on the text and what they are learning, but instead they have to keep looking up to find out what the question is before they write again. It also splits the teacher's focus. Making a PowerPoint actively impedes my lesson preparation. I'm thinking about slides instead of thinking about content. I might put 20 questions on a PowerPoint, but actually I need to be thinking about 100 questions to ask pupils verbally. Teachers need to spend time planning those micro-questions as well, not just the few 'big questions' pupils might answer at length in discussion or writing.

Finally, technology. Hands up who has ever had technology fail them in the classroom? That'll be every teacher ever. And it's awful. You stand there at the front. You have nothing. You could write your questions on the tiny actual whiteboard that is awkwardly positioned so not all kids can even read it, but then you'd have your back to the children and we all know how that pans out. Plus, what if half your questions are about the gorgeous images you've meticulously selected? You've got nothing. You do a little dance. You pray you can contain them.

A few years ago, I was teaching a poem by William Carlos Williams called 'Landscape with the Fall of Icarus.' It's a poem inspired by a painting by Pieter Brueghel, so obviously I felt I needed to show the kids the image in order for them to understand the significance of the poem. I cued the image up ready. And then it transpired that my board was not connected to my computer. I panicked. Technical assistance could not arrive in time, so I taught that lesson without my picture. I just explained the picture, and why it was important. The kids got it, wrote about the poem; happy days. It was fine. But by the afternoon my board was fixed. So, the second time I taught the lesson to the other year 7 class I taught, I had the image ready to go.

And it was a much weaker lesson. We had split attention. We had a request to pull the blinds down so they could 'see it properly.' They were confused by other aspects of the picture I didn't want them to focus on. It was, all in all, a massive distraction.

So, what's the alternative?

The two-page lesson

I suggest teachers simplify their resources for each lesson into two pages. This constraint feels manageable for teachers and pupils. It cuts down on time photocopying and handing out. It means children are faced with the same format each lesson, which I would argue is a good thing. Far better for children to know what is coming in each lesson: the lives of teenagers, in particular, are so endlessly dramatic, the last thing they need is a 'surprise' in the form of geography. (I would also argue that no amount of 'fun' activities in any lesson will come close to competing with the joys of YouTube and iPhones, so why bother? Oh – not to mention that children learn more this way – 100% focused on the task and the learning.)

The second reason it's great to use two pages is for posterity: after the first year of planning lesson to lesson, simply package up your two-page lessons one after the other, and you have a teacher-made textbook. Add on a front cover, and then each lesson is a two-page spread – children don't even need to turn the page during the lesson, if you're worried about wasting the two seconds it would take to do that. You can tweak this teacher textbook from year to year; you can share it with colleagues in your department. It is versatile.

So, what should be contained in these two pages? Again, keep it really simple.

Reading

The bulk of the two pages should be text for the children to read that is specific to your subject. The more children read, the more knowledge they will have of their subject. They will also absorb the *style* of writing in your subject. I will always remember the Head of Science at one school complaining that the children always wrote stories; they couldn't 'write like a scientist.' But the children were also taught in PowerPoint format, with information distilled into bullet points. If they weren't *reading* science it is easy to see why they could not *write* scientifically.

The amount of reading you require of your students each lesson will vary depending on the ability of the pupils and their age. If including less text, you may choose to break that text up with images, or put the text in a larger font. That said, avoid having low expectations. You might always put some of the text, perhaps the less vital parts, in italics as a cue to you that you will only read it if you feel the class can handle it. Turn on line numbering in your computer's writing software, so when you read as a class and break off to explain, you can just say: 'line 18' and everyone knows where they are again.

Questions

Once you've got the text in place, you need to add some questions. This is where you're thinking about how to get children to think about the material in question. I'd group your questions into two types: comprehension questions and application questions. Don't discount basic comprehension questions. Too often, we take for granted that pupils have understood what is happening in a text, perhaps because we as children were under-challenged and remember comprehension questions as ludicrously simple. For high-attaining sets, you can simply ask these comprehension questions orally and see what response you get. If they're struggling, then focus more on explaining the text, and get them all to write their answers to these questions. You can have comprehension questions spread throughout the text, but that is quite a high-effort strategy from the outset and may be something you add to later iterations of your teacher textbook. The simplest and quickest way to plan is to simply include five comprehension questions at the end of the text. Then, perhaps under the word 'extended writing' or 'extension' or 'application' or 'analysis,' have one to three more challenging questions that get the children to practise the key skills you want them to have picked up during the lesson's reading and discussion.

So, what you have at its simplest form is text and some questions, pre-prepared. During your lesson preparation, I would suggest reading over the material and annotating it yourself with what you think the children will struggle with. You might also add questions you want to ask them. Save this annotated sheet, as it can help you to improve your teacher textbook for next time.

Examples

The other thing you may wish to include is an example paragraph which illustrates to the children what you expect them to be able to do. They might be tasked to annotate that paragraph themselves, or you could go through it together and highlight the key aspects. This isn't crucial – to save time, you may wish to write this paragraph together 'live.' If you do this, type it out on a Word document you save entitled 'Unit 1, exemplars.' That way, again, the next year you can save workload and embed these examples into your booklet. Display your screen on the board and narrate your thinking so children can understand how you have created this paragraph. I actually think that live writing is the best way of sharing exemplars with a class, because it allows the children to hear your thinking as you compose the answer, but for the sake of new teachers, or weaker teachers, or non-subject experts using your booklet, it would be helpful for these to be included in future iterations.

You might also create 'non-examples' to help the students recognise what they need to do to improve. Again, this can be something you do retrospectively, perhaps using an example from a student's book revealing a key misconception. Type it out, display it, and ask the students to correct it – again, saving the document to work it into your workbook as 'non-examples.'

Recaps

Finally, I would include a recap at the start of the two-page lesson. We'll go into more detail about lesson starters in the next chapter, but the basic idea is this: work out the key stuff you want the children to remember for the long term during this unit. Break it down into 20 or so chunks of knowledge. Then, at the start of each lesson, ask five questions about this core knowledge. Stick these at the start of your two pages, and make them as simple as possible – preferably requiring one-word answers (though this is not always appropriate – again, more on that next).

Booklets

So, what you should have in your planning is this: two pages. Five quick, snappy recap questions at the top. About a page to a page and a half of text, with line numbers. Five comprehension questions at the bottom. One to three application or analysis questions following on from that. You've packaged this up to fit on two sides of A4 paper, and so you simply print 30 copies of that out and hand it out to your class. If you're super organised, you might print a whole week's worth of lessons, and hand them out on the first day. If you do that, remember to number the pages so you can direct the children each lesson. It really is that simple, and it even works for sixth formers, though the questions you might ask of the sixth form may well be significantly more challenging.

Then, when you come back to prepare that unit to teach the following year, you simply copy and paste each two-page document into one document, add a front page, add page numbers, and press print. If you've got a bit more time to invest, you might use your annotated pages (paper clip these together as you go) to add some comprehension questions scattered through the text (perhaps put these in italics if they are intended purely as oral questions), and perhaps embolden words or concepts pupils struggled with in the lesson at the time as a cue to whoever teaches it next to focus on those aspects. Maybe copy and paste some of the exemplar and non-exemplar paragraphs you have created throughout the year. If you had a final assessment for the unit, perhaps type up the best one and put it in the back of the unit for future reference, or to help your next cohort of kids prepare for that assessment.

I would very much discourage using PowerPoint, but if your subject is one which requires colour images which are large (art, sources in history, and so on), have one PowerPoint for the unit and label the bottom of the screen clearly. Then, in your improved booklet, you can direct the teacher to 'slide 11: image of the Madonna.'

What is not included in this booklet is one massive aspect of teaching: feedback. Don't worry – there's a whole chapter on feedback coming up. The booklet is intended to be simple.

In the following pages are some example early-draft lessons, with some explanations from subject experts on why particular choices have been made. These lesson plans are also available as two-page downloads from www.routledge.com/9781138488649.

ENGLISH

Although this is an introductory lesson to a GCSE text, the class in question had previously studied Gothic fiction, so the recap is intended to activate students' prior knowledge. Each aspect of context has been chosen because it has the clearest applicability to the text, and will be revisited throughout the unit. The final questions are inspired by *The Writing Revolution*, which you can read more about in Chapter 7.

Context

Recap

1 When did Gothic fiction become popular?

2 What does 'duality' mean?

3 What Gothic **texts** or authors do you remember?

Extension: What Gothic **features** do you remember?

The *Strange Case of Dr Jekyll and Mr Hyde* is a Gothic **novella** (short novel) by Robert Louis Stevenson. First published in 1886, it tells the story of a scientific experiment which goes horribly wrong. In attempting to split his personality, Dr Jekyll creates an **alter-ego**, Mr Hyde, who does terrible things and becomes more and more out of control as the novella goes on. Over time, critics have wondered whether Mr Hyde might be **symbolic** of a number of things.

Reputation

In Victorian society in the nineteenth century, reputation was extremely important. People were expected to keep to a certain moral code and value system. Throughout the novel, Jekyll aims to preserve his reputation just as Hyde destroys his. The acceptable behaviour of Victorians could mask hidden moral corruption. Victorians loved reading about shocking behaviour, and a **genre** of literature called the 'shilling shocker' became very popular.

Science

The nineteenth century saw **rapid** scientific developments. In 1859, Charles Darwin published *On the Origin of the Species*, which introduced the idea of **evolution** for the first time. His work was threatening to religion, because Christians believed that God made all human beings, and the idea that humans had evolved from **primitive** animals was frightening to them as it challenged their entire world view. In the novella, another scientist called Dr Lanyon represents science as something which is **rational** and **explainable**, while Dr Jekyll's science is seen as morally unacceptable.

Duality

At the centre of the novel we have one man split in two: Dr Jekyll is also Mr Hyde, though it takes the characters some time to work this out. In many ways, the novella explores the idea that all humans are essentially **dual** in nature: we all have good and evil within us, and often suppress one side or the other. The narrator of the novella, Utterson, tries throughout the novella to explain the mystery of Hyde, attempting to find a **logical** explanation. Yet, his thirst for logic denies him realisation of the truth.

The concept of duality is also present in science. The **psychologist** Sigmund Freud had begun to explore the theory of consciousness: the id, the ego, and the superego. The ego is the man; the superego the way he wishes to be seen by the world. The id is the hidden desires of man – man's subconscious, innermost feelings.

The Victorians were keenly aware of religious duality: in the Bible, Lucifer, God's brightest and most loved angel, begins a war against him and is cast down to hell to rule there as the Devil, or Satan. Victorian Christians recognised that all humans have both good and evil inside them, and they had to make the decision to choose the good. In the novella, Jekyll refers to the soul as a battleground between the **angelic** and **fiendish** sides of humans.

Crime

With London's expanding population and the amount of people experiencing gruelling poverty on the rise, crime exploded. Previously, people had lived in close-knit communities where everyone knew each other's name. Now, though living **physically** close together, London provided a new **anonymity**.

Between August and November 1888, the impoverished **Whitechapel** area of London was the scene of five brutal murders. The killer was dubbed 'Jack the Ripper.' All the women murdered were **prostitutes**, and all except for one were horribly **mutilated**.

There has been much speculation as to the identity of the killer. It has been suggested that he or she was a doctor or butcher, based on the evidence of weapons and the mutilations that occurred, which showed a knowledge of human **anatomy**.

Jack the Ripper was never caught and he is not thought to have killed again after November 1888. For Victorians, the possibility of a highly educated murderer spoke to their fears of the **dual** nature of man: both good and evil.

Gothic

Early Gothic novels focused on the **supernatural** and were often based in foreign countries and in **ancient** settings like castles. But in the nineteenth century, Gothic authors turned their attention closer to home and began to write novels set in familiar locations. 'Jekyll and Hyde' is set in London.

Nineteenth-century England experienced **rapid** change. Along with scientific discovery, there were more and more factories which changed the face of London and other major cities. London's population expanded from one to nearly seven million between 1800 and 1900 as part of the **Industrial Revolution**. People were unsettled by the new way of city life: the over-crowding, the way rich and poor lived side by side, the pollution and the crime; 'Jekyll and Hyde' explores some of Victorians' deepest **anxieties** about their capital city.

Many Gothic novels around the time of 'Jekyll and Hyde' explore the idea of an **alter-ego**: published in 1818, *Frankenstein*, by Mary Shelley, tells of a scientist who creates a gruesome creature which comes to represent all his greatest fears, and in Oscar Wilde's 1890 *The Picture of Dorian Gray*, a man's portrait begins to symbolise the **deterioration** of his soul. In 1824, James Hogg wrote *The Private Memoirs and Confessions of a Justified Sinner*, which tells the story of a man pursued by his own double self.

Questions

Answer in full sentences. You do not need to use quotations. Use all your own words.

1 What is the story of *Strange Case of Dr Jekyll and Mr Hyde*?

2 Explain the importance of reputation for Victorians.

3 How was scientific discovery seen by many Victorians?

4 What does 'duality' mean, and how is it **relevant** in 'Jekyll and Hyde'?

5 In what ways does 'Jekyll and Hyde' relate to other Gothic literature at the time?

Extension: Why did Stevenson choose to set his novella in London?

Finish the sentence three times in your book

1 Victorian London was unsettling because . . .

2 Victorian London was unsettling, so . . .

3 Victorian London was unsettling, but . . .

Jon Field, Vice Principal and science teacher at The Ebbsfleet Academy

Students in my science class are given a sheet like this for every lesson, which is hole-punched and clipped into their books with treasury tags. The lesson starts with starter questions recapping the content from the previous lesson. These require students to access their memories, which in turn helps to reinforce those memories. The lesson purpose is clearly stated so that students know *what* they are about to learn; I don't give reasons *why* they are learning as I see the knowledge as an end in itself. The lesson is then broken into two chunks that follow the same format: text introducing new ideas followed by comprehension questions that test their understanding of those ideas. The lines of text are numbered so that I can point students towards help without giving them the answers, and to help me manage the lesson. I try to write in a 'formal-ish' voice, being disciplined with, and modelling the use of, technical vocabulary, whilst keeping the language and tone accessible and human. Whenever new words are introduced, they are defined immediately, clearly and directly without requiring inference from the context of the sentence. When modelling a process (such as determining the charge of an ion), I give multiple examples of gradually increasing difficulty that are all explained in the same way. In terms of delivering the lessons, I typically select students to read the text to the class, whilst the rest of the class reads along with them in time. I then project the lesson on my whiteboard and talk back through the content, focusing on the key ideas, elaborating on the more difficult concepts and using techniques such as 'I-say-you-say' and 'choral response' to reinforce memories and test understanding. As we do this, students are expected to annotate the sheets to help make more sense of them. The comprehension questions always directly assess understanding of the information in the text to ensure that key ideas are understood; I do not ask any questions (other than the challenge) for which the answer cannot be gained from the text. Process- and calculation-based questions gradually ramp up in difficulty to build confidence. There is always a challenge question designed to stretch more able learners. After each lesson I reflect on the delivery and if needed I tweak the lesson to improve the bits that didn't work well, or to include the good explanations that I might have improvised during the lesson, so that over time the lessons continually improve.

C5 LESSON 2 – IONIC COMPOUNDS

Starter questions (answer on this sheet)

1 What is an ion?

2 What is a cation?

3 How are cations formed?

4 What is an anion?

5 How are anions formed?

6 What is an ionic bond?

7 What is the name of the force involved in an ionic bond?

Lesson purpose: To determine the formulae of ionic compounds and describe their structure.

Working out the formula of an ionic compound

Ionic compounds always have the same number of positive and negative charges; this means that although the ions in them have positive and negative charges, overall, the ionic compound has no charge because the positive and negative charges cancel each other out.

Common ions

Group	Charge	Examples
1	1+	Lithium, Li^+; Sodium, Na^+; Potassium, K^+
2	2+	Magnesium, Mg^{2+}; Calcium, Ca^{2+}
3	3+	Aluminium, Al^{3+}
5	3−	Nitride, N_3^-; Phosphide, P^{3-}
6	2−	Oxide, O_2^-; Sulphide, S_2^-
7	1−	Fluoride, F^-; Chloride, Cl^-; Bromide, Br^-

Polyatomic ions

Ion	Formula
Ammonium	NH_4^+
Hydroxide	OH^-
Nitrate	NO_3^-
Sulphate	SO_4^{2-}
Sulphite	SO_3^{2-}

To work out the formula of an ionic compound, we have to decide how many cations and anions we need to balance out their charges.

■ **Example 1: sodium chloride**

- This is made of sodium (Na^+) and chloride (Cl^-) ions. The positive charge on the Na^+ is balanced out by the negative charge on the Cl^-, so we just need one of each and the formula is *NaCl*.

▩ Example 2: potassium oxide

● This is made of potassium (K^+) and oxide (O^{2-}) ions. K^+ has one positive charge whilst O^{2-} has two negative charges, so we need two K^+ ions to give us two positive charges to balance out the two negatives. The formula is K_2O.

▩ Example 3: aluminium nitrate

● This is made of aluminium (Al^{3+}) ions and nitrate (NO_{3-}) ions. Three NO_{3-} ions are needed to balance the three positive charges on the Al^{3+}, but because NO_{3-} is a **polyatomic ion** (ion with more than one atom) we need to use brackets to show this: $Al(NO_3)_3$.

▩ Example 4: aluminium oxide

● This is made of aluminium (Al^{3+}) and oxide (O^{2-}) ions. In this case, the three positives and two negatives will not work nicely together, so you should look for the lowest common multiple of the charges: $2 \times 3 = 6$. This tells us we will need two Al^{3+} ions ($2 \times 3^+ = 6^+$) and three O^{2-} ions ($3 \times 2^- = 6^-$), so the formula is Al_2O_3.

You can also use these ideas to work out the charge of ions that you don't know. For example, with $FeCl_2$, because you know that there are two negative charges ($2 \times Cl^-$), the iron (Fe) ion must have two positive charges to balance this out, so it is Fe^{2+}.

Comprehension 1 (answers in your book in full sentences)

1 Why do ionic compounds have no overall charge?

2 Determine the formulas of the following, and explain your reasoning for each one:

   a Lithium fluoride

   b Lithium oxide

   c Magnesium chloride

   d Calcium nitrate

   e Ammonium sulphite

   f Magnesium nitride

3 Potassium phosphate has the formula K_3PO_4. What is the formula of the phosphate ion? Explain your reasoning.

4 **Challenge:** Draw a flow chart that can be used to help determine the formula of ionic compounds.

Ionic lattices

The ions in ionic compounds arrange themselves in a three-dimensional arrangement called an **ionic lattice**. An ionic lattice is a repeating pattern of alternating positive and negative ions, all held together by the electrostatic forces (attraction) between the opposite charges. In a single grain of salt, this pattern is repeated about a million times in every direction. This causes most ionic compounds to form **crystals** – pieces of a material, like diamond, with a geometric shape, straight edges, and smooth surfaces – because the ions line up in such a regular pattern.

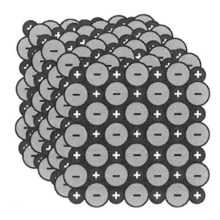

Comprehension 2 (answers in your book in full sentences)

1 What is an ionic lattice?

2 Draw and label a square two-dimensional diagram of the lattice arrangement of a 16-ion piece of potassium bromide.

3 Why do ionic compounds form crystals?

4 **Challenge:** A single grain of salt (NaCl) contains about 1.2×10^{18} ions and is roughly cubic. How many ions could you fit along the length of a single side of the cube? How many of these ions are sodium ions? Explain your reasoning.

Lucy Newman, lead humanities teacher as part of the teaching and learning team at Oasis Academy South Bank

This is a GCSE lesson. The recap is intended to activate students' prior knowledge. The questions have been put throughout the text to help break up the reading for the students. Questions 1–11 could be answered verbally or written in their books depending on the need of the class.

This lesson was written by Head of Humanities, David Barnes, and edited by Lucy Newman.

TITLE: WHY DID ENGLAND GO TO WAR WITH SPAIN IN 1585?

Recap

1 Mary was executed because of Elizabeth's Parliament and advisors, for example . . .

2 Mary was executed because of involvement in foreign plots against Elizabeth, for example . . .

3 The three causes of the Revolt of the Northern Earls 1569 were . . .

4 The Act of Supremacy 1559 changed church leadership, for example . . .

5 The Act of Uniformity 1559 changed church services, for example . . .

Cause 1: a marriage proposal

Philip II of Spain had been married to Elizabeth's Catholic sister, Queen Mary. After Mary died, Philip proposed to Elizabeth. In 1559, Elizabeth turned Philip down. Philip was deeply disappointed as he had hoped that the marriage would ensure England remained Catholic and that he would control the country. Philip was also disappointed because he had hoped to bring England into an alliance against France. A marriage would have made the prospect of any future war between Spain and England very unlikely. At this time marriage was more about power alliances between countries than love. Despite Elizabeth having turned Phillip down, Spain and England remained on good terms for a number of years.

1 Who had Philip II of Spain previously been married to?

2 Why did Philip want to marry Elizabeth?

Cause 2: religious differences

The massive religious differences between Spain and England became obvious with Elizabeth's Religious Settlement of 1559. King Philip of Spain was a strong Catholic. He regarded Elizabeth's Protestant Church as a great evil. Philip believed it was his life's work to return countries to the Catholic faith. In 1571, the Pope excommunicated Elizabeth and called for Catholic monarchs to act against Protestant England. However, even though Philip hated the idea of a Protestant England, he took no direct action for over 25 years.

3   What denomination was England at this time?

4   What denomination was Spain at this time?

5   What happened in 1571 that encouraged war between Catholic and Protestant countries?

Cause 3: piracy

English sea captains sought to participate in the West Indian trade and were attacked by Spanish coast guards. In retaliation the English sailors began to make money by attacking Spanish treasure ships. These ships carried gold and silver from the mines of South America back to Spain. Such piracy made a lot of money for England. Even Elizabeth unofficially supported these voyages in return for a share of the riches! This angered the Spanish, who made several complaints to Elizabeth. Francis Drake was regarded as the most famous of all English pirates. In 1572, he stole silver worth £20,000 (about 30 million at today's prices). An even bigger haul came in 1579 when Drake stole £140,000 worth of cargo from a Spanish cargo ship – the *Cacafuego*. However, these events took place years before war finally broke out in 1585.

6   What did the English steal from Spanish ships?

7   Elizabeth encouraged this because . . .

Cause 4: events in the Netherlands

Philip also controlled territory in the Netherlands. In 1572, Protestants in the Netherlands rebelled against Catholic Spanish rule. One of the leaders of the rebellion was **William of Orange**. People from the Netherlands are called Dutch people. William Prince of Orange was angry at Spanish persecution of Dutch Protestants and believed people in the Netherlands should have freedom of belief. In 1578, Philip sent a massive army, led by the **Duke of Parma**, to the Netherlands. The Spanish soon began to restore their control over the Netherlands. Parma was made Governor of the Netherlands. He was responsible for many things including taxation. In response to Spanish aggression William asked the French **Duke of Anjou** to help fight the Spanish. However, the Duke soon made himself unpopular with the Dutch people and was forced to leave in 1583. In 1584, **William of Orange** was assassinated and it looked like the Protestant rebels were finally about to be defeated. Elizabeth consequently faced an important decision. If she did not send troops to help the rebels then the Spanish would have control of the Netherlands. This would also mean that a large Spanish army was based just a few miles across the Channel from England. In 1585, Elizabeth signed the **Treaty of Nonsuch** and sent an army of 7000 to help the rebels. The army was under the command of the **Earl of Leicester, Robert Dudley**. Leicester was quite unsuccessful and argued with his Dutch allies. Despite this, he did slow down the progress of the Spanish army.

This direct military involvement by England enraged Spain. To them, it seemed like the English were laying claim to the Netherlands. **This was a key moment and Philip immediately began plans for an invasion of England.**

Complete these statements.

8   The leader of the Dutch rebellion was called . . .

9   The denomination of the Dutch leader was . . .

10   William Prince of Orange was not happy with Spanish rule because . . .

Answer the question:

11   Who did William ask to help him fight the Spanish?

Further statements to complete:

a   Piracy made the Spanish very angry, but was not the most important cause of war because . . .

b   The rejection of Philip's offer of marriage was not the most important cause for war because . . .

c   Religious differences were not the most important cause of war between England and Spain in 1585 because . . .

d   The events in the Netherlands led to conflict between England and Spain because . . .

e   The most important cause for war with Spain was . . .

Naveen Rizvi, maths curriculum advisor at United Learning

For me, a typical maths lesson starts with a recap exercise. This strengthens pupils' memories; something called **the retrieval effect**. It takes about the first five minutes of the lesson.

Next I start teaching **something new**, but it's the resource preparation that happened *before* the lesson that guarantees this will be successful!

To prepare those resources, I start by mapping out the content of the unit. I am teaching pupils how to write the **reciprocal** of a **fraction**, an **integer**, or a **mixed number**.

So next, for each of those, I try to list every **type** of question or activity a pupil could be given.

I'd class finding the reciprocal of 3/7 or 4/7 as the same 'type,' whereas finding the reciprocal of 3/7 or 7/4 are a different type, since, this time, the second task shows that we can find the reciprocal of a fraction even when the number on top is bigger than the number on the bottom.

Once I've listed all the question types, I prepare some worked examples, but as well as thinking about 'what **examples**' I'll include, I think carefully about 'what

sequence' they need to be presented. So, in this lesson, the first worked example I use shows pupils explicitly how the first fraction, 5/4, becomes its reciprocal, 4/5. Then, the second example explicitly communicates the concept of reciprocal applied to a slightly different context: same numbers, but starting with the bigger number on top. This also shows that the process of converting a fraction into its reciprocal works the same in both directions. Then, the next examples are less explicit cases such as finding the reciprocal of an integer or a unit fraction.

The sequence of examples is as important, if not *more* important, than the examples themselves. Each new example is guaranteed to be understood **only** because it represents a small, discrete, but meaningful step forward in understanding, compared to the previous.

The goal of the example sequence isn't just for pupils to understand and follow *these* specific examples, but for them to develop a **generalised strategy** for applying the concept in a diverse range of contexts; transferring it further, and further, eventually into complex forms of problem solving.

So, the sequence of worked examples and exercises will continue to expand, across lessons, and pupils will see me model solutions to increasingly tricky problems, rather than abandoning them in the hope that they'll 'discover' the methods they need for themselves.

After teaching this initial sequence, pupils attempt a mini quiz, responding to questions on mini whiteboards. This quiz is one type of formative assessment which checks pupil understanding, allows me to clear up any confusion, and ensures that both pupils' written work and final result are 100% accurate. The questions are designed so pupils are practising what they are most likely to struggle with when working independently. So, this part of the lesson allows me to give precise and actionable feedback to pupils.

Next, pupils start an independent task, which they complete in their books. At this point I circulate the room, making sure to prioritise my weakest pupils.

The goal of a well-crafted sequence of worked examples, followed by the mini whiteboard questions, is to allow pupils to complete their independent work with minimal errors, and without needing much, if any, support from me – in other words, to help them be truly independent!

Finally, in the last stage of this lesson, I connect the concept of 'a number's reciprocal,' to a related, key, fact: that if you multiply a fraction by its reciprocal then the result is always 1. This is a fact that is often overlooked, and rarely taught.

To communicate this fact, I prepare worked examples and mini quiz questions that eventually connect what was taught earlier in the lesson to this new fact. This both consolidates what has been taught previously, and allows pupils to apply it to yet another new context.

It is imperative to **directly teach** the hardest applications of a concept; otherwise, pupils are likely to encounter a negative and demoralising experience of failure. Conversely, by sequencing content so it starts with the basics, and then escalates the difficulty and complexity ever so carefully, it's instead possible to create experiences where all pupils are successful in learning even the most challenging content.

RECIPROCALS

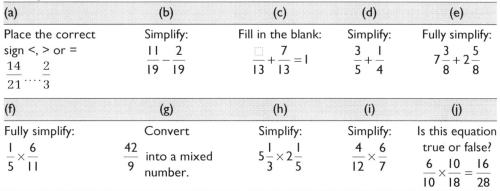

Recap

(a)	(b)	(c)	(d)	(e)
Place the correct sign <, > or = $\dfrac{14}{21} \cdots \dfrac{2}{3}$	Simplify: $\dfrac{11}{19} - \dfrac{2}{19}$	Fill in the blank: $\dfrac{\square}{13} + \dfrac{7}{13} = 1$	Simplify: $\dfrac{3}{5} + \dfrac{1}{4}$	Fully simplify: $7\dfrac{3}{8} + 2\dfrac{5}{8}$

(f)	(g)	(h)	(i)	(j)
Fully simplify: $\dfrac{1}{5} \times \dfrac{6}{11}$	Convert $\dfrac{42}{9}$ into a mixed number.	Simplify: $5\dfrac{1}{3} \times 2\dfrac{1}{5}$	Simplify: $\dfrac{4}{12} \times \dfrac{6}{7}$	Is this equation true or false? $\dfrac{6}{10} \times \dfrac{10}{18} = \dfrac{16}{28}$

Worked examples

We have learnt how to multiply fractions. We are now going to learn how to multiply a fraction by another fraction to equal to 1. When we multiply a fraction by its reciprocal the result is always 1. Before we learn how to multiply fractions to equal to 1, we will learn what a reciprocal is.

Here are a few fractions and their reciprocals:

$$\dfrac{5}{4} \to \dfrac{4}{5} \qquad \dfrac{4}{5} \to \dfrac{5}{4} = 1\dfrac{1}{4} \qquad \dfrac{1}{4} \to \dfrac{4}{1} = 4 \qquad \dfrac{1}{2} \to \dfrac{2}{1} = 2 \qquad 2 = \dfrac{2}{1} \to \dfrac{1}{2}$$

Mini quiz

I Write the reciprocal for each of these fractions.						
(a)	**(b)**	**(c)**	**(d)**	**(e)**	**(f)**	**(g)**
$\dfrac{7}{10}$	$\dfrac{7}{9}$	$\dfrac{1}{9}$	$\dfrac{1}{10}$	9	19	$\dfrac{1}{19}$

What if we are trying to find the reciprocal of a mixed number? We firstly write the mixed number into an improper fraction, then write it's reciprocal. Here are some examples:

$$1\dfrac{1}{4} = \dfrac{5}{4} \to \dfrac{4}{5} \qquad 3\dfrac{3}{4} = \dfrac{15}{4} \to \dfrac{4}{15} \qquad 1\dfrac{1}{3} = \dfrac{4}{3} \to \dfrac{3}{4} \qquad 1\dfrac{1}{2} = \dfrac{3}{2} \to \dfrac{2}{3} \qquad 2 = \dfrac{2}{1} \to \dfrac{1}{2}$$

Mini quiz

2 Write the reciprocal for each of these fractions.						
(a)	**(b)**	**(c)**	**(d)**	**(e)**	**(f)**	**(g)**
$1\frac{7}{10}$	$1\frac{7}{9}$	$1\frac{1}{9}$	$2\frac{1}{9}$	9	$\frac{1}{9}$	$\frac{3}{9}$

Practice exercises

1 State the reciprocal for each fraction; give your answer as an improper or proper fraction.						
(a)	(b)	(c)	(d)	(e)	(f)	(g)
$\frac{2}{3}$	$\frac{2}{5}$	$\frac{2}{10}$	$\frac{10}{2}$	$\frac{12}{2}$	$\frac{2}{12}$	$\frac{2}{1}$
(h)	(i)	(j)	(k)	(l)	(m)	(n)
2	$\frac{2}{7}$	$\frac{7}{2}$	$\frac{7}{11}$	$\frac{4}{11}$	$\frac{11}{4}$	$\frac{1}{4}$
(o)	(p)	(q)	(r)	(s)	(t)	(u)
$\frac{6}{4}$	$\frac{4}{6}$	$\frac{1}{6}$	$\frac{6}{1}$	$\frac{6}{10}$	$\frac{10}{6}$	$\frac{10}{1}$
(v)	(w)	(x)	(y)	(z)	BONUS	BONUS
10	12	$\frac{12}{17}$	$\frac{1}{17}$	17	$\frac{17}{11}$	$\frac{1}{11}$

2 State the reciprocal for each fraction; if your answer is an improper fraction then write it as a mixed number.						
(a)	(b)	(c)	(d)	(e)	(f)	(g)
$1\frac{2}{3}$	$1\frac{2}{5}$	$\frac{2}{5}$	$\frac{2}{10}$	$\frac{1}{2}$	$2\frac{1}{2}$	$2\frac{2}{3}$
(h)	(i)	(j)	(k)	(l)	(m)	(n)
2	$2\frac{2}{7}$	$1\frac{2}{7}$	$\frac{7}{11}$	$\frac{4}{11}$	$2\frac{3}{4}$	$2\frac{1}{4}$
(o)	(p)	(q)	(r)	(s)	(t)	(u)
$1\frac{2}{4}$	$\frac{4}{6}$	$\frac{1}{6}$	$\frac{6}{1}$	$1\frac{6}{10}$	$\frac{10}{6}$	$1\frac{1}{6}$

Worked examples

We have learnt how to find a reciprocal for a fraction. We will now learn about a fraction and its reciprocal and the magical relationship they have. If we multiply a fraction and its reciprocal the result will always be 1. Here are some examples:

$$\frac{5}{4} \rightarrow \frac{4}{5} \qquad \frac{4}{5} \rightarrow \frac{5}{4} = 1\frac{1}{4} \qquad \frac{1}{4} \rightarrow \frac{4}{1} = 4 \qquad \frac{1}{2} \rightarrow \frac{2}{1} = 2 \qquad 2 = \frac{2}{1} \rightarrow \frac{1}{2}$$

$$\frac{5}{4} \times \frac{4}{5} = \frac{20}{20} = 1 \qquad \frac{15}{4} \times \frac{4}{15} = \frac{60}{60} = 1 \qquad \frac{1}{4} \times \frac{4}{1} = \frac{4}{4} = 1 \qquad \frac{1}{2} \times \frac{2}{1} = \frac{2}{2} = 1 \qquad \frac{2}{1} \times \frac{1}{2} = \frac{2}{2} = 1$$

What if we have a fraction multiplied with a missing fraction and the result is equal to 1, how do we find this missing fraction? We can use our knowledge that a fraction multiplied by its reciprocal will equal to 1. Here are the steps to find the missing fraction:

1 Write the reciprocal of the fraction.

2 Check that the multiplication of the top numbers and the bottom numbers result in the same number.

$$\frac{5}{4} \times \frac{?}{?} = \frac{20}{20} = 1 \qquad \frac{15}{4} \times \frac{?}{?} = \frac{60}{60} = 1 \qquad \frac{?}{?} \times \frac{4}{1} = \frac{4}{4} = 1 \qquad \frac{1}{2} \times \frac{?}{?} = \frac{2}{2} = 1 \qquad \frac{?}{?} \times \frac{1}{2} = \frac{2}{2} = 1$$

Mini quiz

Find the missing fraction for each of these calculations.				
(a)	**(b)**	**(c)**	**(d)**	**(e)**
$\frac{7}{10} \times \frac{\square}{\square} = 1$	$\frac{4}{10} \times \frac{\square}{\square} = 1$	$\frac{\square}{\square} \times \frac{4}{10} = 1$	$\frac{\square}{\square} \times 4 = 1$	$\frac{\square}{\square} \times \frac{1}{4} = 1$

Practice exercises

3 Write the reciprocal of each fraction, and show that its multiplication with its reciprocal equals to 1.

(a)	(b)	(c)	(d)	(e)	(f)	(g)
$\frac{2}{3}$	$\frac{2}{5}$	$\frac{2}{10}$	$\frac{10}{2}$	$\frac{12}{2}$	$\frac{2}{12}$	$\frac{2}{1}$
(h)	(i)	(j)	(k)	(l)	(m)	(n)

3 Write the reciprocal of each fraction, and show that its multiplication with its reciprocal equals to 1.

2	$\dfrac{2}{7}$	$\dfrac{7}{2}$	$\dfrac{7}{11}$	$\dfrac{4}{11}$	$\dfrac{11}{4}$	$\dfrac{1}{4}$
(o)	(p)	(q)	(r)	(s)	(t)	(u)
$\dfrac{6}{4}$	$\dfrac{4}{6}$	$\dfrac{1}{6}$	$\dfrac{6}{1}$	$\dfrac{6}{10}$	$\dfrac{10}{6}$	$\dfrac{10}{1}$
(v)	(w)	(x)	(y)	(z)	BONUS	BONUS
10	12	$\dfrac{12}{17}$	$\dfrac{1}{17}$	17	$\dfrac{17}{11}$	$\dfrac{1}{11}$

Worked examples

If we multiply a fraction and its reciprocal the result will always be 1. What if we have a mixed number? We have an additional step where we must convert the mixed number into an improper fraction before we find the reciprocal of that fraction.

Here are the steps to find the missing fraction:

1 Convert the mixed number into an improper fraction.

2 Write the reciprocal of the fraction.

3 Check that the multiplication of the top numbers and the bottom numbers result in the same number.

$1\dfrac{1}{4} = \dfrac{5}{4} \rightarrow \dfrac{4}{5}$	$3\dfrac{3}{4} = \dfrac{15}{4} \rightarrow \dfrac{4}{15}$	$1\dfrac{1}{3} = \dfrac{4}{3} \rightarrow \dfrac{3}{4}$	$1\dfrac{1}{2} = \dfrac{3}{2} \rightarrow \dfrac{2}{3}$	$2 = \dfrac{2}{1} \rightarrow \dfrac{1}{2}$
$\dfrac{5}{4} \times \dfrac{4}{5} = \dfrac{20}{20} = 1$	$\dfrac{15}{4} \times \dfrac{4}{15} = \dfrac{60}{60} = 1$	$\dfrac{4}{3} \times \dfrac{3}{4} = \dfrac{12}{12} = 1$	$\dfrac{3}{2} \times \dfrac{2}{3} = \dfrac{6}{6} = 1$	$\dfrac{2}{1} \times \dfrac{1}{2} = \dfrac{2}{2} = 1$

Mini quiz

Find the missing fraction for each of these calculations.

(a)	(b)	(c)	(d)	(e)
$1\dfrac{7}{10} \times \dfrac{\square}{\square} = 1$	$1\dfrac{4}{10} \times \dfrac{\square}{\square} = 1$	$\dfrac{\square}{\square} \times 1\dfrac{4}{5} = 1$	$\dfrac{\square}{\square} \times 4 = 1$	$\dfrac{\square}{\square} \times \dfrac{5}{4} = 1$

Practice exercises

4 Write the reciprocal of each fraction, and show that its multiplication with its reciprocal equals to 1.						
(a)	(b)	(c)	(d)	(e)	(f)	(g)
$1\frac{2}{3}$	$1\frac{2}{5}$	$\frac{2}{5}$	$\frac{2}{10}$	$\frac{1}{2}$	$2\frac{1}{2}$	$2\frac{2}{3}$
(h)	(i)	(j)	(k)	(l)	(m)	(n)
2	$2\frac{2}{7}$	$1\frac{2}{7}$	$\frac{7}{11}$	$\frac{4}{11}$	$2\frac{3}{4}$	$2\frac{1}{4}$
(o)	(p)	(q)	(r)	(s)	(t)	(u)
$1\frac{2}{4}$	$\frac{4}{6}$	$\frac{1}{6}$	$\frac{6}{1}$	$1\frac{6}{10}$	$\frac{10}{6}$	$1\frac{1}{6}$

Now that we've looked at the resources we'll be using for each lesson, let's head a little more deeply into the way we begin a lesson, both in terms of what we use and how we use it.

Put simply

- Instead of an attention-splitting PowerPoint, make one single resource for students and teachers.

- Instead of making multiple resources, condense each lesson to two pages for simplicity and focus.

- Instead of burning the midnight oil trying to come up with 'fun' activities, annotate your resource with the questions you will ask to check the children are learning.

5 Starting a lesson

There has long been a compelling argument against seeing the 'lesson' as the unit of time to plan for student learning. Rather than planning learning into pre-decided 50-minute chunks, the argument goes, we should be prepared to stretch or compress the way we are covering material as the children require it. I think the teacher-made textbook outlined in Chapter 4 allows for this: if you don't get to the end of a two-page lesson, you can always just keep going the following lesson. If you race through one two-pager, well – that may be an issue the first time you teach the two-pager, but the following year when it's all packaged into a handy booklet, you can simply turn the page to the next lesson and plow on.

Daily recap

I would always advocate planning a daily, or lesson-ly, recap of the unit you are covering into your resources. In addition to this, though, I would also think about additional recap questions to begin your lesson. We've already explored how pupils learn: they need to commit knowledge components to long-term memory, which frees up working memory to process new ideas. We also know that the more students are quizzed on a concept, the more likely they are to commit it to long-term memory.

The other important concept governing the way we start a lesson is that pupils learn by connecting new information with existing knowledge. So, if we begin a lesson with a well-chosen recap, we are activating that prior knowledge, and making it much more likely they will be able to understand any new concepts being introduced.

To do this simply, you need to have a really clear and organised idea of what the specific things are in your subject that you want your pupils to remember for the long term. Once you have this, you simply need to write it down, and ask the pupils about it again and again and again. We know that the most effective way to commit something to memory is to be tested on it: simply rereading or being told is not enough. When we struggle to bring something from our memories to the forefront of our minds, it strengthens the neural connections surrounding that idea. The more times we bring it to the front of our minds, the more likely we are to remember it long term. (Just remember trying to learn all your colleagues' names on the first week of a new school. The first day is a nightmare. Day two you are really struggling to connect names and faces. Some people's names and faces start to stick. Before you know it, you're remembering the humans you interact with without having to even try. You've committed this new knowledge to long-term memory, which frees the rest of your mind up for focusing on your job!)

Behaviour

Before going into the resourcing around starting the lesson with a recap, it's worth reiterating the message of Chapter 2: that nothing you plan as a teacher really matters if no one is listening to you. So it's important to get behaviour right at the start of a lesson.

Ideally, your school has shared expectations. Pupils may line up outside a classroom, they may file in silently, they may stand behind their chairs, they may sit down and start working straight away. Whatever these whole-school expectations, even if you disagree with them, you must follow them. By all means, give feedback through your line manager about why you think the school system doesn't work or how it could be improved. But remember that schools work best when everyone does the same thing, and this is never more the case than in terms of expectations around behaviour.

If your school has no such shared expectations, the path of least resistance is this: pupils come in straight away, sit down straight away, and work in silence. Anything else is going to be difficult to enforce: getting children silent in a corridor of other noisy children is tough, and getting them standing behind their chairs silently is also tough. Far easier to have them come straight in and sit down and start working in silence. At least that way, you are giving them something to focus on which is not having a chat with their friends. In a school lacking systems, your classroom is your haven, and it will be easier to enforce silence as each pupil comes in. Embed the expectation that they work straight away doing something they always do – which I suggest in this chapter is a written recap – and then behaviour manage them into getting on with it.

If you have a whole-school responsibility for behaviour, however, I might suggest you enforce lining up silently before filing in silently. It is far easier to begin a lesson when all pupils arrive simultaneously. If this is a whole-school expectation, corridors become much easier to manage, as while you reinforce a silent line your colleague next door is doing the same. In already very loud corridors, though, again this may be basically impossible. If corridors are a battleground in your school, first tackle whole-school behaviour in lessons, and get the kids in quickly.

Setting expectations

If you have a 'difficult' class, or one proving difficult for you in their previous lesson, it is worth reinforcing behaviour expectations at the start of the lesson. Call the class to attention and remind them of your expectations. Do this positively. Emphasise that you want them to focus so they will learn. Remind them that they succeed or fail as a team, and you're not prepared to let the minority overpower the majority. Always remember that, even in the most challenging school contexts, *most children are doing the right thing*. As a new teacher, it's hard to see this sometimes. If you're someone who thinks the 'whole class' has been awful, challenge yourself at the end of one lesson to write down the names of every child who was basically doing the right thing basically all the time. You will be surprised with how many names you write down. The naughty kids are most obvious, but rarely most numerous.

When you reset expectations, you need to definitely *not* alienate that silent majority who are doing the right thing. Definitely *don't* make sweeping negative statements. By all means, anonymously speak about the 'small minority' who did 'X, Y, and Z' last lesson. If you're going to increase the sanctions on offer, flag this up at the start of the lesson. ('Last lesson, I gave warnings for calling out. That did not work. Too many of you were *still* calling out. This lesson, calling out will result in a *straight detention*. That is so the majority of you who want to learn can do so. You have been warned: if you call out, you will receive a detention straight away.') Children are hyper-sensitive to what is and is not fair. If your line manager or mentor has told you to have harsher sanctions and higher standards, explain this to the class. That said, never give the impression that you disagree with these rules: make it clear that these are *your rules* that *you* are enforcing.

Recaps

Once your class is ready to learn, start your lesson with a recap. The easiest way to do this is by verbally saying the questions and getting the children to write their answers. I'm a big fan of getting every child to write for a few reasons. Firstly, if you rely on hands up, you can be sure that some children aren't going to bother to think. Even if you use 'hands down' questioning, they can always not listen and say 'I don't know' if you call on them. Secondly, in general, children could do with reading and writing more in lessons, and I would seize any opportunity to get them to write a bit more, especially when this takes so little time. Finally, silent, focused writing is a great way to set the atmosphere of your classroom. That said, for the sake of speed, you may choose instead to recap orally as this takes much less time, if you are pressured for time.

Starting your lesson with a recap is, as I said previously, the best way to strengthen a child's retrieval strength of new knowledge. The other benefit to always beginning your lesson with a recap is that it feels safe. Any time you do something consistently as a teacher, your children feel safer. 'Oh Ms So-and-So's class – we always come in and write for five minutes, answering questions about what we've already learned.' They know what they're getting. It's like coming home. The other huge benefit of recaps on learning is that, hopefully, most of the children should be achieving 100% in them. That is your aim. If most children are achieving two or less out of five, you're pitching it too high, or you haven't taught them securely enough initially. When most children in your class start the lesson with five out of five (and ask for hands up: 'who got five out of five? Amazing!'), they begin the lesson feeling like winners. Feeling like they can do it. And nothing motivates like success.[1]

So what exactly should you be recapping on? To begin with, start with what is most familiar: the current unit of learning. For each unit, you should have an A4 page – no more, but sometimes perhaps less – of key knowledge you want the children to remember for the long term. You might get the children to initially learn these as homework, though I would advise always reading them through together to ensure they fully understand each concept – blind parroting of terms is *not* the end goal. At the start of each lesson, you have a copy and the class has a copy. Simply work your way through the sheet, asking the next five questions. Notice which questions children are often getting wrong, and ask those more frequently. Try and ask questions which have one-word, or short, answers, so the recap can be rapidly done. If you must ask questions with longer answers, this might be a good moment to do the recap orally instead of in writing. You definitely don't want to be 20 minutes into the lesson having simply asked five questions of recap.

You should then mark the recap. I would get children to mark this themselves, ideally using a different-coloured pen. This is especially important if you are in a school with a marking policy – your line managers will enjoy seeing lots of ticks in different-coloured pen, and it may take some of the heat off you. (We'll go into this more in the final chapter, on feedback.) Go over it rapidly. You may even want to give children the answers yourself, although I would remind them of the question so it can secure their understanding, especially if they have got the question wrong. If you want to take answers, ask for hands up. To get a sense of which questions they struggled with, ask pupils who achieved three out of five to tell you which numbers they got wrong. Take a small sample – perhaps two or three students at most – to get a feel of this. It's not an exact science, and you don't want to create work for yourself unnecessarily.

After you finish the unit recap, move on to a second recap of *previous* units. You might, if you have a very high-attaining set, simply use knowledge organisers from previous units and recap everything. I suspect, though, in 90% of cases you will want to be more selective. After each unit, take a highlighter and work out what is the *very most crucial knowledge*: what is the stuff you want them to know for the *very* long term? If pupils studied poetry in the past, you will want to recap what a simile is, but perhaps not the exact date that William Blake wrote 'The Tyger.' When you choose this core knowledge to recap, you will want to consider the children you are teaching. Those who are really struggling with your subject's basic knowledge will need to go over the core stuff more frequently. Those who are not struggling will be able to remember more. It is a brutal truth to face, but overwhelming struggling pupils with huge amounts of knowledge will not help them. Think about what your worries are for the group you teach: if you worry they won't do well at university, recap everything. If you worry they won't get into university, recap less. If you worry they won't pass their GCSE, then compress the core knowledge even more so you are constantly revisiting the basics. (And remember: just because they are struggling in year 9 doesn't mean they can't fly in year 12. Some children progress at different rates. Giving struggling students a really firm foundation does not mean you are capping their possibilities. In fact, the opposite: it means you are leaving doors open for their futures.)

Key knowledge

Now, we come to the thorny issue of what to choose to remember for the long term. What constitutes the key information in your subject area that children must learn off by heart to be able to truly excel? Unfortunately, as with earlier comments in Chapter 3 on curriculum choice, there is no consensus on this. We need to base our decisions on a few key ideas.

Firstly, though perhaps most depressingly, what do pupils need to know to pass a GCSE in your subject? Considering that most children will take at least a GCSE in your subject, this seems like a good area to begin with. This is, of course, especially pertinent if you are considering years 10 and 11. For these year groups, it is actually quite easy: look at the specification, the past papers, the exemplar responses, and the materials children will be learning. Then decide which knowledge has the highest wattage in student responses.

Secondly, what is the core underpinning knowledge pupils need to have in your subject to be able to access everything else? For maths, this might start with number bonds and times tables. For art, this might be colour theory. For history, it may be a sense of general chronology. This will likely be added to the knowledge you want to revisit with pupils, especially the weakest pupils, again and again.

Then, you need to package up this key knowledge into a format that is easily used by both students and teachers. I would use a knowledge organiser for this purpose.

Knowledge organisers

I was first introduced to the concept of knowledge organisers by Joe Kirby, who has written with typical clarity on their use on his excellent blog.[2] The concept is a series of grids forming no more than one A4 page. Each grid has two parts: a term, and a definition or explanation. The explanation must be one short, simple sentence. For each term, give it a number. That way, if you have a weaker class, you might stage the numbers in difficulty, and you can therefore tell a class to 'learn 1–4' instead of all items listed at once. Or, you might get a class to learn half of a grid for two consecutive weeks of homework.

Each grid should be grouped into an overall idea. In English, this might be 'characters,' or 'plot,' or 'techniques.' In history, it might be 'concepts,' 'dates,' and 'monarchs.' In maths, it might be 'terms,' 'instructions,' and 'sequences.' Whatever the main overall ideas are, you use those to group your grids. It is vital to keep the terms and definitions short for the same reason it is vital to limit yourself to one A4 page: the idea is the students will commit *everything* on this grid to memory, so we want to make it as easy as possible for them to do so. If you use this resource across a whole school, remember that students may learn six units in six subjects across the year – that's 36 pages of A4 paper's worth of core knowledge. Multiply that by their five years of education, and you have an awful lot already for students to memorise.

Some of this information will be what I call 'short term': stuff that kids *must know* while they study *that* unit, but that isn't readily transferable to other units. You might want to shade this a light grey on your knowledge organiser. The other stuff should be 'long term': the stuff that is transferable between units, or that you want students to remember for the very long term. Perhaps leave that unshaded, giving you the option to highlight the *most key* stuff for your very weakest students.

Knowledge organisers are great, because they mean you have total clarity on what is expected to be learned by all pupils. Teachers inheriting a class or coming new to a school have on a few pieces of paper the things they can *guarantee* children all know. It gives a new teacher tremendous power to quiz pupils on stuff they have done previously, showing their 'omniscience,' even if this is the very first class they have ever taught. The teachers have these, but so too do pupils. When we tell pupils to go home and revise, there is often a real lack of certainty over *what* or *how* to revise. With the knowledge organiser, you can simply say: 'go away and learn everything on knowledge organiser A that is unshaded.'

We are often stuck for what to set for homework. Teachers wrack their brains trying to work out the best task for their students to do. Too often, it is just thought up on the spot, or in moments of pressure. But with knowledge organisers, you can simply set pupils the task of learning one box, or one set of terms, or the first five terms. Perhaps have them use 'look, cover, write, check' to do this, and take in a piece of paper with their notes on it to ensure they have done it. Better still, test them on it the following lesson, and instead of punishing for lack of handed-in homework, you can punish those who fail the test. (At one school I worked at, we used to only sanction the weakest three in the class, always taking into account pupils who really struggled. It is surprisingly easy to tell who has simply not put effort into learning, and who has genuinely struggled. You can use your knowledge of them in class to guide your judgement.)

Used in this way, knowledge organisers are sort of like 'flipped learning,' where the hard work of students learning information is transferred to them personally, and so less time can be used for teacher guidance and explanation, as well as student practice of the key skills required in that subject.

But, as I've mentioned briefly, we should not only expect students to learn the knowledge organiser for homework. To do so would be to render it essentially useless: students will then be able to parrot back to you a definition with no real understanding of what it means. No: instead, you need to *teach* the knowledge on the organiser to students. Depending on what is encoded there, you may do this up front in a unit, or you may do this a little bit at a time. With complex information, crucial information, and with weaker cohorts you will want to explicitly teach content multiple times, as well as checking for understanding. Otherwise, you will only ever have pupils with surface knowledge, and miss capitalising on a core benefit of using knowledge organisers: deep understanding of core knowledge.

To make a knowledge organiser, you need to have the unit of work before you. The first thing to do is decide on the content you will teach. Once you have the content, consider the key areas of that unit. Then find between five and ten, but ideally not more than 12, concepts for each key area. Write these on one column and their definition in the opposing column.

The process of making a knowledge organiser will look different dependent on your subject, so we'll walk through a few examples now.

Hilary Samuels, head of history at the Ebbsfleet Academy

When making our knowledge organisers in the history department (see example on page 70), we always start by creating the assessment, considering what skills we are trying to develop and what knowledge will be required. For this topic, I decided that we wanted to prioritise the development of an argument, so I focused on the question of what contributed most to the passage of the Representation of the People Act of 1918. I always include key concepts and key dates in history knowledge organisers, to give students the foundation of core knowledge. We shade in grey the optional sections, which I would expect all students to attempt but not necessarily commit fully to memory. We also include week numbers so that if a student is absent they do not fall behind but instead know exactly what to revise.

For this specific topic, we decided that the key topics were the actions of the suffragists, the actions of the suffragettes, and the impact of WWI, so the vocabulary and dates reflect these priorities. We chose to include some more general vocabulary relating to democracy, as well as a lesson on the topic, to give our students the broader political awareness to enable them to put this topic into context. We also include quotes on our knowledge organisers to bring the history to life for students, so that they can use the language of the time and support their arguments with more specific evidence. Similarly, the two compulsory individuals are ones without which the students could not write their essays. The two additional individuals would add a level of political depth to essays for those who hope to achieve the top marks. Finally, for the notes on Millicent Fawcett we chose to include her role in higher education; although this is not directly relevant to the enquiry question overall, this provides a useful opportunity to discuss university and career aspirations with the year 8 students.

Elisabeth Bowling, head of English at Hethersett Academy

In sitting down to create the knowledge organiser shown on page 72, I started with the 'what' and the 'why': what I wanted the pupils to learn, and why I felt this was important. This unit for year 9 was designed to mirror the requirements of the GCSE poetry specification, but be more rooted in the experience of the pupils in focusing on the poetry of their city. Although the poems in the organiser are ordered thematically rather than chronologically, I wanted to retain a diachronic view of poetry. For me, it was crucial that the pupils learned about the development of poetry through time with a clear sense of poetic movements, from Romanticism through to Modernism. I wanted the pupils to develop a sense of progression and influence in poetry, as well as prepare them for a higher study of literature at A-level.

In selecting the terminology for the knowledge organiser, I focused firstly on form and structure rather than language. This helps children read poems as a whole entity, rather than immediately feature spotting at sentence level. The grammar section worked as part of a year-long grammar strand. The 'skills' section, perhaps problematically named, was useful in establishing the expectations of this unit for pupils and teachers.

After making several versions of the organiser that were densely packed with information, dates, context, and interpretations, I decided to massively pare it down to the relatively simple version here. The first reason for this was practical: this organiser was to be printed on the back of their A5 anthology booklets and more text would make it off-putting. However, I came to see the best knowledge organisers as the mere 'bones' of learning; the core structural knowledge needed to support pupils' readings and interpretations of the poems. These bones would then be brought to life through the in-depth study in class.

Jon Field, Vice Principal at the Ebbsfleet Academy

In science, our knowledge organisers are larger than in some other subjects due to the sheer volume of factual knowledge in the Combined Science syllabus that we teach. We had difficulty reducing this to a set of core facts that all students must know, because beyond the absolute basics (What are particles? What is a cell? What are forces?) there isn't any particular aspect of the syllabus that is deemed especially important or worthy of assessing by the exam boards. This approach provides us with knowledge organisers that are very comprehensive – you would probably achieve a grade 9 if you fully memorised them – but they also risk overwhelming the students. To solve this problem, each item on the knowledge organisers is given a difficulty rating – from one to three stars – so that students can focus first on the one-star material before ramping up the difficulty as their confidence improves.

To write the knowledge organiser shown on page 73, I worked through each of the lessons my department had written for this part of the syllabus and pulled out the key facts, writing these in as concise a form as possible. At times, the content of the lessons goes beyond the exact detail laid out in the specification, because either it was interesting to teach or we had seen examples of exam questions addressing it. In these cases, there was a judgement to be made about exactly what to include and some knowledge was excluded.

On balance our knowledge organisers probably have more knowledge than is required, but we decided better this than the opposite! As time, and the examinations cycle, moves on and we become more confident about exactly what can and can't be examined, it is likely that we will prune our knowledge organisers to cut out some of the excess, the first candidates probably being the items about Henry Moseley.

After the recap, you'll move on to the bulk of the lesson. Thinking back to our resource, the first thing the children will do after that recap is read some subject-specific material, so that's what we'll look at next.

THE

Ebbsfleet

A C A D E M Y

Aspire, Excel

Year: 8

Term: 2b

Topic: Votes for Women in the United Kingdom

Key concepts

W1		
Democracy	A system of government by the whole population or all the eligible members of a state.	
Suffragists	People who support the extension of suffrage, especially to women.	
Election	A formal and organised choice by vote of a person for a political office or other position.	
WSPU	The Women's Social and Political Union, led by Emmeline Pankhurst.	

W2		
Suffragettes	Activists in the British WSPU, led by Emmeline Pankhurst, who used methods such as hunger strikes.	
Vote	A formal indication of a choice between two or more candidates or courses of action. Usually expressed through a ballot or a show of hands.	
NUWSS	The National Union of Women's Suffrage Societies – an organisation of women's suffrage societies in the UK.	
Campaign	A series of operations intended to achieve a goal, confined to a particular area or style of fighting.	

W3 – Key Individuals

John Stuart Mill	A member of the Liberal Party, he was the first MP to call for women's suffrage. He first presented a petition in 1866.
Millicent Fawcett	She was a moderate campaigner. She wanted to improve women's opportunities for higher education and in 1875 co-founded Newnham College,

Key Dates

W4– 1832	Mary Smith presented the first women's suffrage petition to Parliament. The Great Reform Act was passed.
1867	A petition was presented to Parliament by MP John Stuart Mill to get women included in the Second Reform Act. It failed. The Second Reform Act was passed and gave the vote to working-class men.

Lesson Sequence

1. To explore how working-class men gained the vote.
2. To understand the timeline of events in the course.
3. To explore the actions of the suffragists.
4. To compare the suffragists to the suffragettes.

	Cambridge. She was president of the NUWSS from 1897 to 1919.
Emmeline Pankhurst	She was a suffragette. She founded the WSPU, which became known for its physical confrontations.
H. H. Asquith	The Liberal Prime Minister of the UK from 1908 to 1916. He opposed votes for women throughout his time as Prime Minister. He did eventually come around to support women's suffrage in 1917, by which time he was out of office.

Quotes

1999, Time	Referring to Emmeline Pankhurst – 'She shaped an idea of women for our time; she shook society into a new pattern from which there could be no going back.'
Emmeline Pankhurst, 'My Own Story'	Men make the moral code and they expect women to accept it.
Emmeline Pankhurst, speech in 1908	We are here, not because we are law-breakers; we are here in our efforts to become law-makers.

1884	An amendment to the Third Reform Bill, to include women in the vote, was rejected.
1897	The NUWSS formed.
1903	Emmeline Pankhurst set up the WSPU with her daughters Christabel and Sylvia.
1905	The militant campaign began. 'Deeds, not words' was adopted as a slogan.
W5–1908	300,000–500,000 people attended a mass rally in Hyde Park. The Prime Minister did not respond. The suffragettes smashed windows in Downing Street and chained themselves to railings.
1909	Hunger strikes and force-feeding began.
1913	The 'Cat and Mouse' Act was passed. Emily Davison died after being hit by the King's horse.
1914	WWI began. Campaigning stopped.
1917	Electoral Reform Bill passed.
1918	Representation of the People Act is passed.
1928	Amendment to the RPA of 1918.

5 To investigate Emily Davison.
6 To explore the impact of the outbreak of war.
7 To revise for the key assessment.
8 To complete Key Assessment 4.
9 To explore women voting around the world.
10 To feedback on Key Assessment 4.

Core Texts	**Key Assessment 4:**
• KS3 History – 'Industry, Reform and Empire' Britain 1750–1900 • KS3 History – 'Technology, War and Identities'	Exam-style paper using sources, on how women gained the vote in England.

The poetry of London: Knowledge organiser

Poets and their poems

Introductions: Benjamin Zephaniah, 'The London Breed'

The city at night: Amy Lowell, 'A London Thoroughfare at 2am,' D.H. Lawrence, 'Town in 1917'

London's outsiders: James Berry, 'Beginning in a City, 1948,' Ralph McTell, 'Streets of London'

Romanticism in London: William Blake, William Wordsworth, John Keats

A London lament: George Eliot, 'In a London Drawing-Room,' T.S. Eliot, 'The Wasteland'

A London celebration: George the Poet, 'My City'

Poetic movement

Romanticism: 1790–1850. A movement inspired by nature, art, freedom, and the belief that poetry should be enjoyed by everyone.

Victorian: 1837–1901. Poetry of this period is often about the struggle of the working people.

Modernism: 1890s–1950s. Modernist poetry broke with previous traditions of form.

Skills

Memorisation: Applying poetry to long- term memory.

Annotation: Analysing a poem for language, form, and structure.

Interpretation: Giving a personal and supported view of a poem.

Comparison: Finding similarities and differences between at leas- two poems.

Poetic terminology and techniques

Stanza: A section or 'paragraph' of poetry

Sonnet: A 14-lined poem about love

Ballad: A poem that narrates a tragic story with a strong rhythm and rhyme

Rhyming couplets: Two lines next to each other which rhyme

ABAB rhyme: Two rhyming lines separated by a line

Rhythm: The beat or pulse

Iambic pentameter: A rhythm consisting of five beats to a line

Free verse: Poetry written with no obvious rhythm or rhyme

Enjambment: When a sentence continues onto the next line

Repetition: When a word or phrase is said more than once

Caesura: A break in a line of poetry

Tone: The general attitude or feel of a piece of writing

Simile: A comparison using 'like' or 'as'

Metaphor: A comparison without 'like' or 'as'

Personification: Giving inanimate objects human qualities

Imagery: Words which create pictures

Assonance: The repetition of similar vowel sounds

Sibilance: A repeated 's' sound

Hyperbole: Exaggerated language

Alliteration: Multiple words beginning with the same sound

Ambiguity: When multiple interpretations are possible

Antithesis: Opposing ideas set next to each other

Grammar

Active sentences: I kicked the ball.

Passive sentences: The ball was kicked (by me).

Verb forms: Present, present perfect, progressive, imperative

Synonyms: Words meaning the same thing

Antonyms: Words meaning the opposite

The language of comparing

Both	However
Similarly	On the other hand
Like	Unlike
This links with	Although
In addition,	Whereas

C3 & 4: Atoms and the periodic table

Lesson sequence

1 Structure of atoms
2 Detailed structure of atoms
3 Isotopes
4 Mendeleev's periodic table
5 The modern periodic table
6 Electron configuration

1 Structure of atoms

*Particle	The tiny pieces that all matter is made from.
*Atom	The smallest independent particle. Everything is made of atoms.
**Size of atoms	About 1×10^{-10} m in diameter.
**Dalton's model of atoms	– Tiny hard spheres – Can't be broken down – Can't be created or destroyed – Atoms of an element are identical – Different elements have different atoms
*Subatomic particles	Smaller particles that atoms are made from.
*Proton	Mass = 1 Charge = +1 Location = nucleus
*Neutron	Mass = 1 Charge = 0 Location = nucleus
*Electron	Mass = 1/1835 (negligible) Charge = –1 Location = shells orbiting nucleus
*Nucleus	Central part of an atom, 100,000 times smaller than the overall atom.

2 Detailed structure of atoms

**Alpha particle	Small, positively charged particle made of two protons and two neutrons.
**Scattering	When particles bounce back or change direction.
**Rutherford's experiment	Fired alpha particles at gold leaf, used a phosphor-coated screen to track where they went.
**Rutherford's results	Most alpha particles went through, some scattered (changed direction).
**Rutherford's explanation	Scattered particles hit a solid nucleus. Most did not hit it; therefore nucleus is small.
*Atomic number	The bottom number on the periodic table; gives the number of protons and electrons.
*Atomic mass	The top number on the periodic table; gives the total protons and neutrons together.
*Number of protons	The atomic number.
*Number of electrons	The atomic number.
*Number of neutrons	Atomic mass minus atomic number.
*Number of protons and electrons	Equal, because each negative electron is attracted to a positive proton in the nucleus.

3 Isotopes

**Isotopes	Atoms with the same number of protons but different number of neutrons.
**Describing isotopes	Mass after the name (e.g. boron-10) or superscript mass before the symbol (^{10}B).
*Nuclear fission	Large, unstable atoms break into two smaller stable ones.
**Uses of fission	Nuclear power, nuclear weapons.
**Relative atomic mass, A_r	The weighted average of the masses of all of the isotopes of an element.
***Isotopic abundance	The percentage of an element that is made of a particular isotope.
***Calculating A_r	– Multiply each mass by the decimal % – Add these up **Note**: decimal % = %/100.

4 Mendeleev's periodic table

*Dmitri Mendeleev	Russian chemist; developed the periodic table.
*Mendeleev's periodic table	Ordered by increasing A_r; some elements switched according to their properties.
*Chemical properties	Includes reaction with acid and formula of oxide.
*Physical properties	Includes melting point and density.
**Gaps in Mendeleev's periodic table	Mendeleev left gaps where no known element fitted and predicted these would be filled with newly discovered elements.
**Eka-aluminium	An element that Mendeleev thought would fill a gap. He predicted its properties, which matched gallium when discovered.

5 The modern periodic table

*Noble gases	Gases that do not react: He, Ne, Ar, Kr.
**Moseley's experiment	Fired electrons at samples of elements and measured x-rays produced.
**Moseley's results	Energy of x-rays produced proportional to the positive charge of the element.

**Conclusion from Moseley's work	The atomic number must be the number of protons in the atoms.
**Pair reversals	Elements (like Ar and K) that are not in order of increasing mass.
**Explaining pair reversals	It means elements should be ordered by increasing atomic number instead.

6 Electron configuration

*Shells	Electrons orbit atoms in shells.
*First shell	Holds up to two electrons.
*Second shell	Holds up to eight electrons.
*Third shell	Holds up to eight electrons.
*Number of electrons	Given by the atomic number.
*Filling shells	Fill shells from the first shell out. Move up a shell when current one is full.
*Electron configuration	The number of electrons in each shell (e.g. Al is 2.8.3).
*Outer shell	The last shell with any electrons in it.
**Groups	Columns in the periodic table; tell you the number of electrons in the outer shell.
**Periods	Rows in the periodic table; tell you the number of electron shells.

Key
Relative atomic mass
Atomic symbol
Name
Atomic (proton) number

Elements with atomic numbers 112–116 have been reported but not fully authenticated

Notes

1 Kris Boulton has a fabulous blog post on how nothing motivates like success: https://tothereal.wordpress.com/2014/06/03/how-tests-teach-and-motivate/
2 https://pragmaticreform.wordpress.com/2015/03/28/knowledge-organisers/

Reading in a lesson

Reading is the single most important aspect of education. I am aware I say this as an English teacher, but I do honestly believe it is true. When children can read at an expert level, a whole world is opened up to them. When children *enjoy* reading and *want* to read, they can choose to enter that whole new world. I really do believe there is no more vital job of the teacher than to ensure all pupils *can* read and *want to* read. And this applies to all teachers, no matter what your subject.

Background knowledge

The reason reading across subjects is so important is that we pick up a lot of background knowledge through general reading. One of the reasons children from middle-class backgrounds do so much better in education is because they have denser general knowledge. Where did they acquire general knowledge? Well, partly parents, partly attending slightly better schools (children in wealthy areas are more likely to be served by Ofsted 'Good' and 'Outstanding' schools,[1] along with high-achieving grammar schools disproportionately attended by children from wealthier backgrounds,[2] added to by the choice of private or state school), and partly their wider background reading.[3]

But reading is not only about fiction. Definitely not. If children *only* read fiction, they will never broaden their knowledge. If we want children to excel in our subject, then they have to *read* in our subject. In a previous chapter, I wrote about the Head of Science who complained that all the children 'wrote stories' in her lessons instead of writing scientifically. When I probed more deeply, I saw that the science lessons were predominantly delivered through PowerPoint slides with limited text. Of course the children couldn't write like scientists – they'd barely read any science.

Added to this is the knowledge that children from poorer backgrounds tend to be ,weaker readers.[4] This is no surprise. The more you do something, the better you get at it, and too many children from disadvantaged backgrounds do not learn to read as a habit at home before coming to school.[5] (There are many, many exceptions to this generalisation, and I know you will meet many, many parents who struggle financially who manage to give their children everything they can in terms of books and reading to them.) The best thing we can do, and this goes for all children but is especially important for our weaker readers, is to ensure they read a lot at school. In fact, I would go so far as to say that children should be reading in *every single lesson* for a *significant portion of time*.

How much should we read?

How much you aim to read with your class will, undeniably, vary. It is true that a very low-attaining class will read far less in an hour than a very high-attaining class. For the most able, I would aim to read at least one and a half sides of A4 at Arial font size 11. For the classes who struggle with reading, I would aim to read one side of A4. For the classes who struggle and are also in a school with challenging behaviour, I would aim to read three quarters of a side of A4. Every lesson. In every subject.

Well, with perhaps two exceptions. In maths, I would read far less, because the crucial thing about maths is that you need to do a lot of practicing of problems to get better at it. When maths teachers ask what children could read in maths, I suggest one paragraph per lesson, and I suggest that that paragraph should be an explanation. The teacher can, of course, simply explain orally to the children, but it's not nearly as good as having it in front of them to refer back to. It's also helpful to new teachers and those who are not subject specialists to have an explanation written by an expert to scaffold their delivery of new concepts to the children.

The other exception should be in P.E. We have a real issue with children becoming increasingly unhealthy in this country,[6] and the last thing those children need is to have a lesson of reading and theory in place of sport. P.E. is not my specialty, but from this uninformed English teacher's perspective, P.E. should really be all about exercising, and not much else. (The caveat to this, of course, is GCSE and A-level P.E., which have not insignificant subject content, and should therefore be considered to require reading as with all other subjects.)

But those of you who teach art can, again, have children reading explanations to supplement oral explanations and demonstrations of technique, or reading on the history of art. Embedding fascinating pages about the artists you are studying into your scheme of work is a great way to get the children to have a deeper cultural understanding of the subject. The same thing goes for drama – why not have children reading some simplified dramatic theory, or about the greatest playwrights who have ever lived? That's not to say you can't have 'practical' lessons in both of these subjects, which are focused on the practice of art or drama. But I do think those 'practical' lessons will be greatly enhanced if you have invested the pupils in reading and understanding more about the subjects.

Reading aloud

You will sometimes be blessed with fluent readers who love to read, volunteer all the time, and do an excellent job of reading in class. Sometimes. It does not happen often, and, in my experience, occurs most usually in high-attaining year 7 classes. Getting children to read aloud can be incredibly difficult. In many schools I have worked in, children simply refuse to read. We need to do two things to counter this.

The first is to make reading aloud an expectation across the school, so children are always expected to read aloud in every lesson. This consistency will really help the classroom teacher. But if you can't do that, you can at least make it a little easier for children. You can add line numbers down the side of the page. You can put the text onto a page of A4 so the font size is comfortable enough for the children to read. (In fact, for lower-attaining pupils you might want to have less text but in a larger font, so perhaps two sides of A4 but size 14 or 15 font.) Inexperienced readers often lose their place, so my colleague Barry Smith, currently Headteacher at Great Yarmouth Charter Academy, advocates having all children use 30cm rulers to follow their place. Having this expectation for all children means they are all supported; if it is 'opt in' children might feel under pressure to look as if they 'don't need' this support. Following along with a ruler is especially helpful for the weakest readers, who find it tough to read silently while a teacher or fellow pupil reads aloud.[7] It also means the teacher can pause the reading frequently to ask questions, check understanding, and elaborate; and the children can save the place where they were reading.

Weak readers

In my fifth year of teaching, I taught the hardest class of my career. As a Head of Department, I had arrogantly supposed I would be more than capable of having the trickiest customers of year 10 in the same room, especially as I knew them so well from having picked them up after being sent out of lessons so frequently in year 9. How wrong I was. The class was an explosive mix of under-confident, under-achieving pupils who genuinely struggled with literacy, but who also sparked off one another emotionally and behaviourally. This class, simultaneously containing some of my favourite pupils I have ever encountered, en masse made me doubt whether I could actually teach. (Once, on sending one child out, she retorted: 'I don't care. You're a crap teacher anyway.' It was on the tip of my tongue to concur. Thank goodness my teacher persona took over or I would have lost them forever.)

The children were painfully weak at reading. One student would auto-correct words she didn't know, rendering sentences essentially meaningless. What she was doing was 'sight guessing': seeing letters and assuming the word. Usually it was a different word to the one written, but she wasn't in the habit of decoding letters to make words. In year 10. It is extraordinary how children can get all the way to their GCSEs and be basically unable to decode accurately. I do think teachers over the years not making their charges read aloud have a lot to answer for. If you don't hear a child read aloud, you don't really know if they can or can't read. You assume a lot from their written answers, which can often be good because they have had a lot of practice listening carefully to ensure they come across as someone who can read. But the basic truth is this: if you never hear a child read aloud, you don't really know if they can or can't read.

With this particular class, I lowered my expectations far too low. I read aloud to them. In fact, I had to practise reading aloud over the summer to be ready for them in September because I had already assumed they were too weak to read themselves. I was a terrible reader. Fortunate enough to begin school knowing how to read, my abilities stalled midway through, and I couldn't seem to move beyond the very simplest texts. I did not read much, except for some truly trashy American 'series' books (*Point Horror*; *The Babysitters Club*). I do not recall at any point having to read aloud in front of a class. In secondary school, my reading repertoire remained limited. Winning a prize for English in year 9, I spent the money on *The Diary of Adrian Mole*, which I'd heard was good. The Head of English was appalled. I recall my first brush with Shakespeare – a valiant year 8 teacher having us perform 'Pyramus and Thisbe' from *A Midsummer Night's Dream*. I hated it. I don't have any memory of reading this play in front of my peers, though it seems likely I did.

Moving into year 10, my memories of reading begin to crystallise. This was the time when anxiety entered. I was, for the first time, becoming truly excited about books, prompted by an incredibly inspiring English teacher, Dr. Byrne. I was also painfully aware of my shortcomings: I'd read a lot, but it tended to be extremely straightforward. Furthermore, where I'd learned new words, I'd learned them by sight, with no idea how to pronounce them. I can't manage to forget, for example, being picked up for saying 'guess-ture' for 'gesture.'

Reading texts I was challenged and absorbed by in class was balanced with abject fear: would I be asked to read aloud? If so, how could I possibly make sure I was pronouncing all the words right and reading at a decent speed and putting enthusiasm into my voice? It seemed impossible. Conversely, I loved reading plays – the shortness of the lines and the space around the text lessened the fear for me.

In short, prior to becoming an English teacher, I had read only approximately 25 pages of text aloud in my life. Surprisingly, this did not seem to be a problem. I was advised during training that students would benefit from 'guided reading,' where they sat in groups and read to one another as I circulated, checking students were on task and understood. The painful exception to this practice was my first year's 10 set 5 (of 5), who were studying *To Kill a Mockingbird*, and seemed unable to read alone in their groups. I valiantly attempted to breathe life into the text, but my shoddy reading skills (among other things) meant disengaged students. (When I finished, a marathon 287 pages later, they applauded. From relief.)

Learning to read aloud

I knew I had to get better at reading aloud, so that summer prior to my fifth year of teaching I practised reading aloud every day. I'd just read four or five pages of the book I was currently reading aloud to myself, or choose a few poems to read. I practised reading one sentence ahead so I could employ the proper intonation to my statements.

By the time I reached my year 10s, I was ready. I read Charlotte Perkins Gilman's *The Yellow Wallpaper* to them. I was so practised by that point that I could do different voices for the different characters. At one point, I even crawled on the floor to mimic the speaker's position. I was very happy with how it was going. I never once asked the students to read.

Then, one lesson, something amazing happened. I was reading aloud, and one of the pupils started reading aloud at the same time as me. As I read the line, she read it at the same time. Now, if I'd had just a little less sleep that night, I might have jumped on the student, assumed she was mocking me, and given her a sanction. Instead, I decided to see where it went. She chimed in with my lines, and I just got quieter and quieter until I stopped altogether. . . . And she carried on.

She read for a sentence or two alone, looked at me, grinned and stopped. I kept reading. Another student chimed in. I got quieter again, letting her read. She read a few sentences, then stopped.

It was, without doubt, the most magical moment of my teaching career to date. The children were telling me not only that they *could* read aloud, but also that they *wanted* to read aloud.

Since then, my thinking about reading aloud has dramatically changed. I have come to realise that the only way we can ever 100% *know* that a child is *actually* reading is if they are reading aloud. If children are not expected to read aloud, they easily can fail to follow the words on the page. Many children are adept at looking as though they are reading, when in reality they are staring mindlessly. We know, too, that the weakest readers need the *most* practice at reading, but are also the ones who tend to volunteer *least* to read aloud, as well as the ones who opt not to read privately after school hours. To serve our weakest readers, it simply *must* be the expectation that *every child can be asked to read aloud at any time.*

Now, it is undeniable that some children will find reading aloud extremely challenging, embarrassing even. It is also true that in some schools where behaviour is not good, children can rightfully fear being made fun of for reading aloud poorly. There are some things we can do to mitigate these circumstances, which I will go into next.

How to read aloud in lessons

First, though, I want to share a method I have found to work brilliantly when reading aloud with pupils. It is taken from Doug Lemov's excellent book of practical pedagogy, *Teach Like a Champion 2.0*, and is called 'Control the Game.'[8] With this method, the teacher reads the text. They then call upon a child to read. The child reads a little. The teacher then picks up the reading.

And that's it. Except, of course, it's slightly more complex than that.

First of all, it's important to start classes off only reading a small amount of text. The amount of text you ask a pupil to read ought to be unpredictable, and it can be between a sentence and three sentences at first. Don't go with an entire paragraph or page, because this becomes too easy for other students to predict. If they know their peer will read to the end of the page, why bother following along? You should indicate the pupil to read with as few words as possible, ideally, just saying their name. Explain this to the pupils before you begin so they know what will happen. If you don't keep your words limited, you can end up spending far too long on every transition. Similarly, when the pupil finishes, don't say much. You might say 'thanks,' but even that *every time* takes up valuable seconds. Those short seconds add up. Definitely don't pause to praise their reading, unless it really was exceptional.

Also embed the expectation that all pupils should be able to read *as soon as their name is called*. This is vital. If there is a long pause for them to find their place, you know they weren't following along, and therefore you know they were not getting the full benefit of the reading you are doing in the classroom. Set up this expectation from the outset so they are aware. Make sure you give the most struggling readers a bit more leeway on this, as they genuinely can find it hard to start reading, even if they were following along. As with everything, if sanctioning, make sure you narrate why this is so important: 'that's a warning, Kieran – if you're not able to read straight away, I know you're not following, and that means you're missing out on vital learning.'

Don't snake around the classroom predictably. Make sure you are calling on pupils at random to read. But I wouldn't use a random name generator – again, it takes up vital seconds of learning time. More importantly, though, it takes the control away from you as a teacher. If you have a very able reader, you can pretty much ask them to read any sentence or group of sentences. But you want to ensure your less able readers meet with success every time, to build their confidence. Select short, simple sentences before you teach your lesson, and underline or highlight these on your own copy. That way, you will know the 'safe sentences' to get your struggling readers to succeed with. With the least confident readers, I might even let them know at the start of the lesson which sentence I am going to ask them to read – at least the first few times. That way, they are prepared and can practise in their head. Yes – they might miss out on a bit of reading in those early lessons while preparing themselves for their sentence, but I think it is worth it for the pay-off of confidence and happiness they receive in return.

If you are reading a page to two pages in every lesson, you can probably expect to hear almost everyone read almost every lesson. If you find you are asking the same children to read, use a class list or seating plan to mark off who has read with a small tick. That way, you can keep yourself accountable for challenging the whole group to read aloud.

Those who cannot read

A small but significant group of pupils in many secondary schools, in particular those in deprived areas, arrive in year 7 being unable to read. By this, I mean they are unable to decode words. For these children, you really do need to do something quite different as a school. I would advise running an intensive phonics programme with these children, ideally in as small a group as you have capacity for. Withdraw them from a couple of lessons a week to do this. In the meantime, though, they can still be in lessons, and, in general, you can usually get them to read very short and simple sentences, although perhaps be aware that they will struggle, and pre-emptively remind your class to always be kind and never laugh at anyone who is making an effort, as 'you wouldn't want to be laughed at yourself,' and so on. I would publicly and strongly punish any child making fun of another child in class. They must know that you will not accept this. If you do this, your classroom becomes a safer space for all pupils to try, make mistakes, even fail publicly, safe in the knowledge that they will be supported by you and their peers.

Reading at home

A word about reading at home. There are many, many expensive programmes out there that claim to track home reading. Some are vastly more effective than others. The reality of the situation is, though, that you will never completely know if a child has read independently at home. Any and all systems I have ever come up with have been 'gamed' by students. Reading logs have been forged. Tests have been taken by siblings and friends. Synopses of novels have been digested to pass even teachers' questioning on a one-to-one oral assessment. If you want to ensure pupils are reading, your only bet is to make them do it with you, as a whole class. That's why things like whole-class reading of a suitable novel with a form tutor or English teacher for 20 to 30 minutes a day are so beneficial. If children have read that much for that long, they will have a massive advantage over their peers.

Any gamification of reading outside lessons, or forced reading outside of lessons, also runs the risk of turning children off reading. Children who love reading will be at an advantage for the rest of their lives. Even if all else goes wrong and they fail all their exams, a child who loves reading has the possibility of future success in a way a non-reading peer will never have. If a child loves reading, they have much more chance of growing up to be an adult who loves reading, and adults who read have the power to pick up their education again. What we must keep at the heart of everything we do as educators is that we want children to be lifelong learners. A well-placed reading programme through subject lessons that supports children with reading is the best way to ensure this happens.

Reading might seem complex, but it's nothing compared with writing. I think I have certainly failed to note the importance of explicitly teaching writing in the past, so I hope the next chapter might provide insights to others like me.

Put simply

- Instead of condensing the text into PowerPoint slides, get the students to read it.

- Instead of silent reading, or reading everything yourself, ensure all children read aloud in class.

- Instead of snaking predictably around the classroom, select students to read unpredictably, and have them read unpredictable amounts so everyone follows along.

Notes

1 On 17 April 2017, the *Guardian* reported: 'Children from poor families are only half as likely to get places in outstanding schools compared with their wealthier peers. . . . Only 15% of children from the poorest 30% of families currently attend a primary school rated as outstanding by Ofsted inspectors, compared with 27% of children from the richest 30% of families. Eleven per cent of children from the poorest families attend a primary school rated as inadequate or requiring improvement, Ofsted's two lowest tiers, compared with 6% of children from the richest households.'

2 The *Guardian*, again, noted on 9 March 2017 that 'While children from the most deprived families in grammar school areas stand only a 6% chance of attending a selective school, the report finds that the most affluent 10% of children have a 50% or better chance of getting into a grammar. For the 1% most affluent, it goes up to 80%.'

3 Daniel Willingham, in *Raising Kids Who Read*, says: 'Research has shown that people with broad general knowledge gained most of that knowledge by reading' (p. 20, Jossey Bass 2015).

4 The report *Ready to Read*, published by the Read On Get On charity in 2015, includes this startling information: 'Children living in poverty face a much greater risk of falling behind – one in three (35%) does not have the language skills expected of a 5-year-old. . . . Good early language skills are even more important for children growing up in poverty – a child who experienced poverty persistently and had below average language skills scores 32% less on reading tests at age 7 and 20% less on comprehension tests at age 11 than a child who never experienced poverty and had above average language skills' (p. 5).

5 The same report notes on page 20: 'It is worrying that poorer children appear to be typically less likely to read for pleasure. Booktrust's reading habits survey has shown that people who never read books tend to live in deprived areas where more children live in poverty. . . .' This is despite a seeming recognition among children from deprived areas that reading widely is hugely important for education: 'New National Literacy Trust research, which for the first time focuses on the reading habits of 8–11-year-old children

as they reach the end of primary school, finds that children from poorer families see the importance of reading: more low-income than higher income 8–11-year-olds see the link between being good at reading and getting a good job when they are older (over 70% compared with 64%). However, it also finds that children from poor families are less likely to read frequently outside of school; less likely to have books of their own; and less likely to read as broad a range of materials – books, magazines and technology-based materials such as text messages and emails – as other children' (pp. 20–21).

6 UK Government report January 2017: 'Childhood obesity: a plan for action': 'Today nearly a third of children aged 2 to 15 are overweight or obese and younger generations are becoming obese at earlier ages and staying obese for longer.'

7 David Didau synthesises a great deal of research on this in his blog post 'The Problem of Reading Along,' concluding: 'reading aloud to students, especially weaker readers, is a good thing to do. . . . *The Problem Comes When Children Are Expected to Follow Along at the Same Speed*. Because they lack the fluency to do this their working memory overloads and derails comprehension.' www.learningspy.co.uk/reading/problem-reading-along/

8 Doug Lemov, *Teach Like a Champion 2.0*, p. 172.

7 Writing

It is undeniable that reading can transform children's lives. Teachers everywhere recognise the importance of reading – both at home and at school – and it is rare to find a parent or professional who isn't clear that reading more can help improve a child's reading skill, along with reading books that are just a *little* challenging but not overly so. In fact, improving a child's reading can seem beguilingly simple, especially when compared with the task of improving writing.

How exactly do we teach students to write better? For years I believed the key was reading: if they could only read more, they would magically become better writers overnight. In some ways, I still believe this. The children I have taught who have been the most accomplished writers have, with no exceptions, also read a huge amount their whole lives.

How do you *teach* writing?

But what about the children who have *not* read a huge amount their whole lives? If they are 11 or 14 years old and poor writers, you simply don't have the time to expect them to be able to absorb how to write well by reading lots. You've got to actually teach them. But how? Schools have invested much time and money in recognising the importance of reading over recent years, but arguably we still need to work harder with writing.

So many teachers share the frustration that their most promising students orally, who seem to have excellent understanding and great insight, seem unable to translate this to words on a page in a coherent and powerful way. Like reading, our children generally need more guidance and more practice than we might imagine in writing.

Practice

Like reading, students should be practising writing for an extended period in every lesson. But of course, it's crucial to break writing down – you can't just set an essay every lesson, because essays demand complex skills and knowledge. Children need the components of long-answer writing broken down, taught, and practised deliberately.

I didn't recognise this when I first started teaching. I realised within a few months of teaching (yes, months – I was too slow a learner in my classroom) that my children struggled to write for extended periods, and that I needed them to have more practice of this. So I introduced 'independent writing.' Every class would end with 20 minutes of answering a question that, I felt, summarised the key learning of the lesson.

There were a number of issues with this. Firstly, I left the writing to the very end of the lesson, which meant that '20 minutes' looked more like ten minutes – or even five – most lessons. Secondly, I hadn't embedded the children's key understanding of the basic aspects of writing, so their writing was littered with errors. I had also omitted to ensure the children understood the most straightforward aspects of the text, so I would see a huge number of misconceptions about character names, context, quotations, and so on.

Writing is complex

But most importantly I had underestimated the complexity of writing an extended paragraph. My students desperately needed me to break down their writing into much more manageable chunks to enable them to experience success in writing. The 'final performance' of writing for an extended period of time is not improved by repeatedly running the 'full show' as it were; it is about a staged build-up of specific tasks that lead to improved performance. As Daisy Christodoulou says, 'The activities which create [detailed, knowledge rich mental models] often don't look like the performance itself.'[1] Although children need practice of writing, it has to be the right kind of practice.

What I had failed to adequately teach was what Doug Lemov calls 'the art of the sentence:' 'ask students to synthesise a complex idea in a single, well-crafted sentence. The discipline of having to make one sentence do all the work pushes students to use new syntactical forms.'[2] We first need children to be able to perfect writing a grammatically accurate, sensible sentence before we present them with the final performance of the paragraph or essay.

Don't knock comprehension

We can conflate this with ensuring students understand what they are learning, and for that we must think carefully about comprehension questions. Many teachers, experts in their field who may well have been gifted in their subject since their own school days, associate comprehension questions with an overly simple and boring activity. Yet, when I first used comprehension questions after a relatively simple text (I thought), I was stunned at how many students had misunderstood crucial aspects of that text. Especially with lower-attaining students, and arguably also with academically strong students who are either very young or grappling with very complex material, comprehension questions are invaluable in signalling to you, the teacher, whether everyone understands what is happening. This is the first stage of learning. If the children don't understand, then they can never go further with their insights – or, if they do, they will not express their ideas with the clarity required for the very top grades.

With weaker students, the beauty of a comprehension question is that the answer stem is located within the question. 'How many wives did Henry VIII have?' requires an answer beginning: 'Henry VIII had. . .' – though even with a simple question like this, I have still had students who had written in the wrong tense at this point, illustrating just how complex accurate writing is for pupils. For some very weak writers, being able to get those first few words down builds their confidence, and enables them to persevere with the information. So I really do believe that comprehension questions should be used much more than they are currently.

Because, but, so

Of course, comprehension questions alone are not enough. One fantastic technique modelled in *The Writing Revolution* is to ask students to finish a sentence three times, using the conjunctions 'because,' then 'but,' then 'so.' By giving students the sentence stem, you then are testing whether they have really understood the fine-grain detail of what they have read, because they must select the appropriate information for what will be three very different sentences. An example given is this:

Sentence stem: 'The Great Fire of London burned 4/5 of the city.'

Because: 'The Great Fire of London burned 4/5 of the city, *because* at the time, citizens didn't have the knowledge or equipment to stop the fire before it spread.'

But: 'The Great Fire of London burned 4/5 of the city, *but* London survived and thrived.'

So: 'The Great Fire of London burned 4/5 of the city, *so* many people had to live in temporary homes until the city was rebuilt.'[3]

Note-taking

Another aspect of writing I'm too guilty of not spending enough time on is note-taking. Again, this is a task that teachers can dismiss as 'obvious,' when to children it is nothing of the sort. The first time I asked students to 'take notes' on something they had read, I was amazed at how many either copied the text out word for word, or, if they managed to use their own words, wrote laboriously in full sentences. Students need to be explicitly taught how to use abbreviations and bullet points, and perhaps we need to over-explain the rationale of taking notes: so that we can assimilate a lot of information at speed. I've found it helpful to model note-taking on the board in real time, and also to spend some time when looking at student work commenting on their note-taking and reinforcing what they might omit in their notes.

Summaries

A few years ago, many schools entered their children for the exam board CIE's international GCSE English Language qualification. Many schools made this choice because of the weighty coursework component, which gave schools a good indicator on entry of the grades their children would eventually end up with. Clearly, coursework is a challenge to the exam system, and too often students in good schools with supportive and educated parents reap the rewards of this compared with their less advantaged peers. That may be, though I would also argue that CIE's iGCSE English contained one of the best English Language exam papers available. It had some very clear and simple questions – and only three of them – which focused children on the most crucial skills they needed to master in writing. One of those skills was summarising. In question three, the children would read a non-fiction text, and write ten bullet points summarising a key detail of that text. They would then turn these bullet points into their summary. It was ingenious in its simplicity, and something I've used ever since when trying to ensure pupils understand the content of a text.

By making the bullet points first (and ten is an arbitrary number; depending on text length, text complexity, and the ability of your class you may go for more or fewer – though too many more and you risk them simply writing out the text verbatim), you force the children to hone in on the key details. By ensuring they write the bullet points in their own words (something the iGCSE did not do, incidentally, but ought to have in my view), you then can see whether they actually understand the text or are just copying.

Summarising is such a vital skill for children to learn – in *The Writing Revolution*, the authors note: 'Having students practice summarising does the following: boosts reading comprehension, helps generate concise and accurate responses to questions, maintains focus on the main idea and supporting details, teaches paraphrasing techniques, provides practice synthesising information from multiple sources, enhances the ability to analyse information, develops the ability to make generalisations [and] aids in retaining information.'[4]

Summarising is a great task to ensure children understand content and can put it in their own words. Being able to write a sentence is the absolute building block of writing, and we must not neglect to teach it. Moving on to paragraphs requires yet more complexity, and, again, breaking this challenging task down into small steps is crucial to support even the highest-attaining students to succeed at it.

How to begin a paragraph

In essay-based subjects, children will need to be taught how to begin their paragraph, and one catch-all term that can apply across subjects is 'topic sentence.' A topic sentence is one that introduces the big idea of the paragraph, encapsulating what the argument will be in it. Explicitly teaching this, across subjects ideally, and then drilling them in writing *just* a topic sentence will really help them when they come to write a full paragraph.

Quotations

Students often struggle when building in evidence or quotations to their paragraphs, so teach them some useful phrases they can draw on. Although these may seem, at first, to curtail students' creative thoughts, these are a crutch they can dispense with – sooner or later – when they are ready. Many children will require that crutch all the way to their GCSEs, and that is absolutely fine, especially if they have four or five go-to phrases they mix around, like 'As Orwell writes,' or even something as simple as: 'in the quotation.' After using a quotation or piece of evidence, with those children who struggle most I would advocate first using the two simple words: 'this means.' This gets students into the habit of paraphrasing the information, proving (to you, and eventually to the examiner) they have understood it. Again, you can begin introducing more set phrases as the course goes on.

Exemplars

Drilling the key components of a paragraph and focusing on these is a great way to ensure students can get the deliberate practice they require before writing their full paragraphs. Following this, reading a lot of exemplar paragraphs and explaining what makes them successful (and then getting the students to annotate and articulate what makes them successful) will help students to visualise the eventual goal of their writing. Exemplars are hard for teachers to pitch accurately, and so in many ways I would always opt to co-write paragraphs in the lesson with my students. This has a few benefits: you can explain your own thinking as you write, so students can hear what you are weighing up as you write the paragraph. You are going much slower, because you are writing, so students have more time to process the information. Finally, and most importantly, you can enlist the help of the class to build the paragraph together, taking suggestions and refining them, explaining your thinking aloud all the time. If your handwriting is terrible, as mine has become, or you don't have a visualiser, or you can't find a board pen (my usual issue) you can simply open a Word document on your computer, set the font size so all can read it, and type away.

As well as 'excellent' exemplars, it can help students to see what *not* to do. I often lift sentences from student books (always anonymised) and display them on the board, asking students to redraft these with a particular focus in mind. To further refine a particular idea, you might want to use exemplars that only require one specific tweak to make them work well – Joe Kirby explains more on these 'minimally different exemplars' in his excellent blog.[5]

Essays

The final stretch of writing is the essay. This final performance requires an unbelievably complex set of thinking, and is much harder for our novice learners than we can ever really imagine. The most important first step of writing an essay is writing a plan.

I'm not sure what happens in primary schools on planning, but every year I encounter students who say: 'I don't plan. Planning doesn't work for me. I've *never* planned,' like they're not 11 years old having written about ten essays, if that, ever. This attitude takes a lot of unpicking and explanation, and sometimes resorting to: 'you will make a plan because I will award marks for the plan and if you don't have a plan you will lose crucial marks.' (Or any variation on: 'you will plan because I say so.') A massive issue in student essays is often a lack of logical argument, and in the absence of a plan their ideas can sprawl incoherently. So talk them through how to make a plan, and by all means make scaffolded 'planning sheets' for your class, even all the way through key stage 3. By key stage 4, you would hope students would be used to this matrix, but if they are not, you may need to continue with the scaffold all the way until their exams, and continue to narrate the elements of a successful essay plan.

Finally, writing a lengthy essay is about the way we structure an argument and the way we structure a paragraph, but it is also about what we know about the topic. When preparing students for a long essay, don't forget to also ensure they are thinking hard about *what* they will say about the topic. The more they know about the topic, the better their essays will ultimately be.

But lessons are not just about reading and writing. The next chapter focuses on talk – the mainstay of almost all lessons.

Put simply

■ Instead of continually writing essays, break down writing into crafting a great sentence first.

■ Instead of assuming students understand, build in comprehension questions as a check.

■ Instead of pre-prepared examples, live-write paragraphs in the lesson and narrate your thinking.

Notes

1 Daisy Christodoulou, *Making Good Progress?* p. 43 (OUP 2017).

2 Doug Lemov, *Teach Like a Champion 2.0*, p. 285.

3 Judith C. Hochman and Natalie Wexler, *The Writing Revolution*, p. xiv (Jossey Bass 2017, Foreword by Doug Lemov).

4 *The Writing Revolution*, p. 139.

5 https://pragmaticreform.wordpress.com/2013/02/02/direct-instruction/ Accessed 22.9.18.

8 Talk in a lesson

So, what of the bulk of the lesson? What comes sandwiched between the recaps and the deliberate practice? Of course, the teaching itself: the explanation. I've already written about the joys and benefits of reading in a lesson, and if you can have a subject expert write an excellent explanation that is read and shared by all students, that is fantastic. But the real magic of teaching comes in the teacher's talk. For students to learn the best, teachers need to instruct them.

Whenever I talk to people about the benefits of direct instruction and teacher talk, oftentimes I have to fight against the characterisation that what I am talking about is 'passive.' I would argue that the best teacher talk is extremely active. In fact, if teachers are simply talking *at* children for long stretches of time with absolutely no engagement, you can be fairly certain the children – if they are normal, ordinary children – are not listening. In the same way that I don't think you can know if a child is actually reading or not unless you hear them read aloud, I also don't think you can know if a child is listening to your instruction unless you ask them questions.

So, the best teacher instruction needs to be highly interactive, and its success depends on a large volume of questions being asked of the children, preferably throughout instruction to check they understand what you are teaching them.

But it is also crucial that children learn to articulate their own understanding of what they are learning. Discussion, therefore, should be the centrepiece of most lessons.

Where talk misleads

What I categorically *do not* mean, though, is that children should talk to one another without teacher input. There are a few issues with doing this, the most pertinent being that too often children do not have the knowledge or understanding to articulate their learning, and if they do so inaccurately to a peer, the peer is then more likely to inherit their misunderstandings. One example that springs to mind from my early days of teaching was when I asked children to tell their partner what they knew about Shakespeare, so that I could then ascertain what their current understanding was. Circulating, I overheard one conversation that went like this:

Child A: Shakespeare was a writer.

Child B: Definitely.

Child A: He lived in Victorian times.

Child B: Yes.

Child A: Which I think means the 1980s?

So, there are two big misconceptions here. The first is that Shakespeare is a Victorian, when of course he is not. The second is that the Victorian age was incredibly recent. This is more usual than we would expect. Chronology is an incredibly complex concept for children to grasp. This is one of the instances that rote learning of dates can begin to assuage, but I leave it to the historians to more fully expound on the best way to ensure children have an understanding of it. Suffice it to say that this experience made me realise that it would be more effective to *tell* the students some information about Shakespeare, using questioning to check their understanding, and then check whether they had understood and remembered it in later lessons.

Group work

At the start of my teaching career, I was a fierce advocate of group work. This was partly a hangover of the preferred Ofsted teaching style being propounded at the time: having group work in your lesson was a dead cert to achieving an 'Outstanding' grade from your observer. The general feeling was that we wanted children to be chatting about their learning as much as possible. I understand where this comes from. Of course, too much teacher talk without breaking it up is difficult for pupils to take in. (I heard of one school that introduced hour-long lectures at key stage 3. I don't know how they implemented it, but I would be extremely wary of such a measure. First-year undergraduates sometimes struggle to stay focused for an entire 60 minutes of listening. Plus, what if the children don't understand what they are hearing? I would be very reluctant to lecture young children with no immediate checks on what they have heard.)

Planning a lesson including group work is difficult. That is part of the reason I think it is, in general, a bad idea to rely on it in your practice. You need to tightly manage it, including transitions. You need to continually call a whole class together, which when you have 30 voices sounding at once is tremendously tricky. You need to monitor what is being said, and intervene with any off-task chat.

All of this is difficult, but not the reason why you should not do group work. The reason you should not do group work is that children need the expert guidance of the teacher to move their learning on. Simply sharing what they already know is open to the risk no one will learn anything.

In my training years, we had the preference to sit a 'high-ability' student next to a 'low-ability' student. In practice, group work becomes the 'brighter' children teaching the less able children. Fine for the less able children, but probably not as good as a teacher. And the more able children were missing out on the opportunity to learn even more.[1]

Children will sometimes come to us with excellent knowledge, sometimes with none, and sometimes with imperfect knowledge. A class discussion is a great way to bounce ideas around while ensuring any misconceptions are caught and corrected immediately by the teacher.

What is the key knowledge?

Class discussion is absolutely vital to learning. Children have to explain what they are learning about, ask questions, and challenge or explore the concepts. If they cannot do that, they will not be able to progress their understanding to its highest level.

When deciding what part of the learning should form the whole-class discussion, let the key knowledge guide you. Look at what you want the crucial learning points of your lesson to be, and make sure you spend most of your time discussing and exploring those. This bears out Willingham's central theme: that we remember what we think about.[2] The aim of your discussion could be one of two, broadly speaking: either to ensure all pupils understand the key concepts, or to enable the students to explore ideas themselves. The latter is especially pertinent in 'essay' subjects, like history, religion and English. Once they have a good solid foundation in the fundamentals, they can then discuss their ideas and suppositions in more depth. This does, of course, depend on a firm foundation of core knowledge. I would hold off exploring ideas in a poem before children understand what a poem is, for example, and how the structures of poems generally work to evoke meaning. They will do best to explore the impact of the language when they understand the basic meaning of the poem, along with the key technical terms involved.

Deciding when and what to discuss, then, is a curriculum question, and should be informed by the choices we make about our curriculum: what is important? What do children struggle with? What do children need to do at a high level for public exams? In terms of pedagogy, you can discuss at any point in the lesson, though I would suggest starting off a lesson with a group discussion might be more of a challenge than it should be. Remember, when pupils come into your room their minds may still be in the last subject – or, worse still, the break-time gossip. Take a few minutes at least to tune them onto your subject with your recap, as explored in Chapter 5, before giving a bit of exposition and introduction, to ensure they are as receptive and thoughtful as possible.

The pitch

Deciding how to pitch your class discussion is probably the hardest part of this section of your lesson. Pitch it too low, and they will lose interest. If you ask questions that are solely knowledge recall, you won't get a discussion going; yet knowledge recall questions can often be invaluable to activate crucial prior knowledge to deepen student responses.

Following that, your questions need to be open enough to allow the children to *apply* their knowledge to new scenarios, to stretch the bounds of their understanding. And yet pitch it too high and you won't find many takers. If your opening gambit is not understood, the children are very unlikely to put their ideas forward. The best bet, I would suggest, is to warm the class up with a few knowledge recall questions, and then start using follow-up questions to those, which you either ask of the same pupil or open out to the classroom.

Ground rules

To have a successful discussion, it is vital that you enforce key ground rules. As I have said previously, the best lesson in the world is essentially pointless if no one is listening. So, before discussing, ensure you have excellent order in your classroom. A vital rule of a successful class discussion, in my experience, is that the teacher fields it. By which I mean, the teacher decides who speaks and when. This is because the teacher is the person in the room who most understands the concepts, and the teacher is also the one with the best overview of which students most and least understand those concepts.

In my experience, if you allow pupils to choose when they speak (which I have seen done in a controlled and calm classroom environment), what you tend to get are the same students speaking. Even when it 'works,' in that it appears calm, polite, and spontaneous, the major downside of this approach is that you have a lot of 'passengers' in that kind of classroom. This is especially true with high-achieving sets, where the ideas of the very 'brightest' can be intimidating to the comparably weaker pupils in that set. If you allow pupils to decide who speaks and when, that gives others a 'free pass' to check out of the discussion.

Instead, the teacher ought to chair the discussion to bring in as many pupils as possible, always with an ultimate aim that everyone speaks. You should be alert to misunderstandings, but don't always feel you have to be the one to correct the child. You might bounce it to another pupil, for example – 'who can explain why Anisa's point doesn't quite work?' Similarly, if a pupil makes a point with which you might agree or disagree, pick a pupil and ask them: 'do you agree? Why?' That said, if the pupil you bounce to also doesn't understand, take this as a cue for you to re-explain to the whole class. Two students not understanding is enough of a guarantee that they aren't the only ones struggling at that moment in the class.

Remember that it benefits everyone to go over key ideas, especially if you sprinkle some questioning into your explanation to engage more pupils actively.

As you chair the discussion, stay positive and upbeat and welcoming. Remember how hard some pupils find it to speak in a classroom setting, and help them feel like they are succeeding. Quash any laughter directed at individuals strictly. Students must feel like your classroom is a safe place for them to make mistakes. If pupils feel they can't make mistakes, then instead of focusing on learning they will be focused on worrying or feeling embarrassed. Seize on any examples of confident pupils making mistakes to remind the class that we learn by working things out, and if we knew everything we wouldn't need to be in school.

With a lower-achieving group, make sure you step up the difficulty of your questioning incrementally. With the very lowest-achieving sets, I have found it helpful to think of this as driving pupils towards the right answer. You ask small questions to which there is very little possibility of them getting it wrong, but through listening to each answer they can start to see the pathway to understanding they may have been missing heretofore. After a time, you will find you need fewer steps. Instead of saying: 'What's the technique in line three and what does it mean?' you would perhaps take it right back: 'Look at line three. Can anyone see a technique there? "My thoughts hissed." Can thoughts *actually* hiss? – No, you're right. So if they cannot *literally* hiss, what technique is this line? – That's right, a metaphor. Now, if Duffy says Medusa's "thoughts" are "hissing," do you think her thoughts are good thoughts or bad thoughts?' This approach takes longer, but it will help children to find success at all levels.

The hallmark of an excellent class discussion is one where everyone contributes and where the learning is moved forwards. Don't be too afraid to follow the discussion, especially with more able groups. If their ideas take them somewhere you had not anticipated, that is not necessarily a bad thing. In fact, it might open up their learning even more. Similarly, if the group gets stuck on a crucial concept, don't be afraid to stop your discussion to reteach it. Always keep in the front of your mind while teaching: what do these children need right now? Then use the tools at your disposal to make that happen.

Once we have read and discussed, the next crucial aspect of the lesson comes into play – and this is perhaps the scariest, because this is the one in which the teacher has to let go and let the children practise independently.

Put simply

- Instead of children explaining to each one another, field the discussion yourself to avoid embedding misconceptions.

- Instead of children working in groups, work as a whole class to ensure all students get the benefit of the expert in the room (you!).

- Instead of the students choosing who speaks, ensure you choose who speaks and when.

Notes

1 If you only ever were using 'bright' as shorthand for 'high prior attaining.' I don't like the idea of 'bright': I think I am a better teacher when I ignore any evidence of innate genetic inheritance of intelligence and assume all intelligence is the result of hard work. If I believe some students are 'just bright,' ultimately I let myself off the hook for the ones who don't achieve. Better to assume everyone can achieve, reach for the stars as a result, and maybe make the moon.

2 'Your memory is not a product of what you want to remember or what you try to remember; it's a product of what you think about.' Daniel T. Willingham, *Why Don't Students Like School?* p. 41.

9 Practice in a lesson

Getting children to practise for an extended period of time may be the most important thing we plan into a lesson apart from instruction. In fact, your teacher instruction, delivery, and explanations may be flawless, but if you do not provide children with an opportunity to practise what they have learned, they will not get better.

What do we want them to practise?

It is important, though, that we consider carefully *what* we want the children to practise: Lemov writes in *Practice Perfect*, the indispensable tome on this theme, 'What you do in practice matters as much as, if not more than, how much you practice.'[1] Many educators argue that what we want to get kids doing is *deliberate* practice; that is, practising a specific skill in a measurable way to help them get better at it. The Deans for Impact report on practice notes five principles of deliberate practice:

1 Push beyond the 'comfort zone.'

2 Work towards specific goals.

3 Focus intently on the practice activities.

4 Respond to high-quality feedback (more on this in Chapter 11).

5 Develop a mental model of expertise (i.e. to know what success looks like clearly, so you know what you are aiming for).[2]

To ensure our students are practising deliberately, we need to think of every activity we plan: what are the children practising when they complete this activity? If we are teaching them the geography of Sri Lanka, and then ask them to create a colourful poster about that country, what are they practising? You might say they are practising designing and attracting a viewer, condensing information to key nuggets. But is that what you *want* children practising in geography?

To work out what you want children to practise, you need to have a strong idea of what you want them to eventually be able to *do* in your subject. In English literature, we eventually want children to be able to articulate their own ideas about a text in seamless prose. In maths, we eventually want children to be able to solve complex equations independently. And so it goes on.

Of any practice you plan, ask yourself: what is the *learning purpose* behind this activity? Ask yourself: does this fit into what I eventually want children to be able to do? Remember, breaking the practice into small steps is crucial. A spelling test may seem small now, but if our eventual goal is that children will write with accuracy, then practising spellings is a worthwhile activity to plan.

Should we differentiate practice?

There is an argument that practice, like instruction, should be differentiated. For some, differentiation of practice means that some children should be given different tasks to other children. I would always argue against such an interpretation of differentiation, because in many instances it means your less able students actually end up falling even further behind. Yet, in instruction, for example, it is true that some children will need multiple exposures to an idea in order to comprehend it, whereas others will 'get it' straight away. Similarly, in practice, some children will need far less of it than other children to reach the same level. This merely means we need to give more time to weaker learners, and perhaps start our explanations more simply and build them up, and break down practice into even smaller steps to ensure they are 'encoding success': that is, practising effectively at each mini-step.[3]

With practice, I would argue that time is the critical factor. Some children will be able to write an essay straight out of the gate – though I suspect fewer than we think. Others will need more time and more steps. That said, in my experience, breaking learning down into too many micro-steps has the potential to overload children, and make an exercise seem more complex than it actually is. Writing a paragraph, for example, has the potential to be infinitely complex. But if our goal is to write a chunk of text answering the question, then it can sometimes be easier for the children to just do their best (remembering most have been writing a generic chunk of text for most of their school career) and then work on improving it after.

The crucial thing with planning practice is that you plan for the children to practise most the things that they are weakest at, and that you ensure that all their practice is feeding into your ultimate goals for what you want the children to accomplish.

Examples of practice

Look again at the resources in Chapter 4, where you will see examples of what the children need to practise in each of the lessons. In English, short-answer questions build up to a lengthier 'extension' response. A similar practice is demanded in the history lesson. In maths, following instruction, lots of targeted questions follow to ensure students can practise what they have been taught.

Put simply

■ Instead of aimless writing, decide what you want students to get better at in your subject and make sure they practise that.

■ Instead of focusing on instruction, build practice into each and every lesson.

■ Instead of making different worksheets, ensure lower-achieving students get more time to practise.

Notes

1 Doug Lemov, Erica Woolway and Katie Yezzi, *Practice Perfect*, p. 21 (Jossey Bass, 2018).
2 Practice with Purpose 2017 Deans for Impact, https://deansforimpact.org/wp-content/uploads/2016/12/Practice-with-Purpose_FOR-PRINT_113016.pdf Accessed 4.18.
3 *Practice Perfect*, p. 25.

10 Ending a lesson

When I was trained to teach, it was assumed that teachers would orchestrate the ending of a lesson, perhaps channelling my childhood music teacher who used to say, 'If you start well and end well, people forget the mess you made of the middle.' Not that we want children to forget the middle of the lesson – quite the contrary – but there is some lingering belief that if we end our lessons with a 'bang,' the learning is more likely to magically stick.

Well, I reject this concept. Think about it from a child's perspective. They push straight on from your lesson to the next, or to break. They go from room to room, bombarded with new information. Perhaps it is reasonable to expect them to retain only a small amount of the multitude of knowledge they have been bathed in, but to assume that magic nugget has to be delivered at the end is a mistake.

It is a mistake because, as Bodil Isaksen says: 'inspiration is not something cultivated by a one-off lesson. It is the product of day-in day-out teaching. . . . Our planning is weakened by lesson-based thinking.'[1] The lesson is the wrong unit of time to be preoccupied with. Children's memories are not formed of 60-minute blocks. We can't expect to package up learning into these bite-sized chunks. To do so would be a lot of hassle for something that is not even proven to be an effective way to learn.

No plenaries please

Please don't say the word 'plenary' to me. It is a made-up word (I know all words were once made up, but this one is definitively biscuit-taking) to illustrate a made-up concept. In the bad old days, teachers were expected to fashion one of these for the end of every lesson. The idea is that they summarise the learning of the lesson and allow teachers to check what learning has taken place. When I trained, we were encouraged to get children to 'reflect' on their learning – not so much *what* they had learned as *how* they had learned it ('how well did you cooperate in your groups, and how could you improve next time?' was a classic Ms Facer question. It almost always resulted in the response: 'listen to each other more,' which was code for 'we shouted as loud as we could for most of the lesson').

But perhaps even more irritating than 'plenaries' are 'mini-plenaries.' Most of these could be renamed 'checking for understanding,' and then you can simply see Chapter 4 on questioning. And that is completely fine. But the difficulty is that these 'mini-plenaries' have been hijacked by people who think they understand teaching and learning (mainly consultants, but not exclusively) and rebranded as the teaching equivalent of the friend who finishes all their Christmas shopping in November. In one school I worked at, we were required to have a mini-plenary halfway through the lesson, and it was to be *one* question which *all* children answered which allowed the teacher to gauge whether the children had understood the first half of the lesson. One question. The genius who can pre-prepare one question at the perfect halfway mark of a lesson, who can then work out how to get every child to answer it, and who can then assess and redirect the lesson, frankly deserves to win teacher of the year, every year, until the end of time. For one lesson in a hundred, I confess, there may be such a single question. But to work this out five or six lessons a day, 39 weeks a year?

It is simply a nonsense. It is not practical and it is not needed. Mini-plenaries need to die a death. Plenaries may as well go with them.

Very few aspects of subjects lend themselves to being packaged so neatly in such small chunks. Concepts are always linked to other concepts, and are, in fact, best understood by children in connection with what they already know, so it stands to reason that to separate a concept out and teach it and test it in isolation is not as helpful as it might at first appear.

Packing away

So, how should we end a lesson? At one school I worked at, it was an absolute revelation. We simply *packed up*. That was the only expectation. Halfway through the reading? No problem. Halfway through a discussion? Still no worries. The kids are writing silently? Still not a problem. Take a quick glance at the clock, realise there are two minutes left (one to three minutes should be plenty to pack away – the more difficult the behaviour, the more time you will need to set aside; first-year teachers with tricky classes might need up to five), call the class together, and announce that the lesson has ended. I'd normally just say, 'that's all for today – we'll pick up again tomorrow.' If, perchance, we were starting a new poem or chapter the following day, I might give a brief trailer for it ('I can't wait to read the most famous war poem of all time with you tomorrow!'), but that's definitely more of a 'nice to have' than a 'need to have.'

That said, even mere packing away can prove more difficult than it should. In a 'challenging' school it is especially difficult. In your average school, you simply need to collect in the books or let the children pack their books in their bags (depending on the expectations). Ideally, have two sensible children you can call on to take in books so you can continue to survey and monitor behaviour. Then give the children instructions to pack away their things – pens, pencils, calculators, and so on need to go in bags. Remind the children that you expect silence during this time – a low murmur might be acceptable in some schools, whereas in others this murmur will soon ring out into a full unwelcome chorus of chat.

I find a countdown very useful when packing away, as children will stretch any time offered when left to their own devices. At one school I worked at, where the expectations were very consistent between classes for packing away, all teachers would count down from 20. I wouldn't call out a full countdown for any more than that. If you give the children a minute, you might say when 30 seconds have passed and reiterate your expectation of what the room will look like when one minute has passed. You could also call out and name children who are ready early as a good example to the others.

The perennial problem with packing away is you're not always sure of how long it will take. This is especially true for new teachers, or when beginning in a new school. To minimise flux, ensure the pupils have complete focus on what they are doing, and do not allow them to stretch the time by asking you questions.

Keep questioning

It is always worthwhile having a few questions to hand, should you wind up with a few spare moments at the end of the lesson after they have packed away. Knowledge organisers, as explained in Chapter 4, are invaluable for this, though you might also take this as an opportunity to lock in the key learning of the lesson you have just taught. A mix of both is probably preferable. This is also a good point to chant poems, times tables, or other core knowledge your pupils have learned off by heart.

And that's it really. A lesson is not the unit of time to focus on as a teacher. Yes, there are lessons where you will have one objective and you will expect the children to master that one objective within that short, defined space of time. But these lessons are vanishingly rare. Instead of focusing on that short chunk, think of the whole unit of learning. Focus on the key aspects you want children to retain and understand from the whole unit, and then at the end of the unit (in addition, perhaps, to the midpoint should the unit lend itself to this) give them a test to see how much they have understood.

So, instead of packaging up your lesson and tying it up with a neat bow, just maximise their learning by moving on to the next thing once they've understood the first thing. Keep it simple.

The final thing to do after the end of the lesson is to provide feedback on the children's work, and that is the topic of the final chapter.

Put simply

- Instead of packaging up each lesson with a bow, just keep teaching.

- Instead of allowing chat packing away, reiterate silence and countdown to keep them moving swiftly.

- Instead of silently standing behind chairs, keep questioning to make the most of every second.

Note

1 Quoted in David Didau, *What If Everything You Knew About Education Was Wrong?* p. 294 (Crown House Publishing, 2016).

Feedback

Clearly, when students write something, it is vital their teachers read it and respond to it. Without feedback, how can students possibly understand where they have gone wrong, or what they need to do differently in the future? Feedback is crucial to the learning process.

Yet, too often feedback is equated with marking. In this chapter, we explore why marking is an inefficient use of teacher time, and cover some ways to give feedback to students that are effective as well as time-efficient. In a profession losing far more teachers than it can afford to,[1] we would do well to think carefully about how to manage workload in the profession, and I contend that marking exercise books is one of the main aspects of workload causing an issue.

Marking is sacred

But marking is also seen as sacred in many education circles. In the words of one Headteacher I met at an interview: 'marking is the most important thing a teacher does. It builds the relationship between teacher and pupil. Without marking, the children will fail.' For many in the teaching profession, marking is still seen as essential to ensure students are held to account. It is seen as the number one way a teacher shows their class they care about them. It is seen as vital to ensuring the children make progress.

Now, I would argue strongly against these assumptions, as indeed I did in the job interview in question (though it must be said, this strategy did not find success in employment terms on this particular occasion). Teachers do not build relationships with pupils through slavishly annotating their writing. They build relationships through chatting to children before and after lessons, showing their personality a bit when teaching lessons, and generally just taking an interest in their charges. They build relationships by turning up and looking like they want to be there. In fact, the exhausted and overworked teacher, I would argue, is less able to build positive relationships with students.

Marking adds to workload

The single biggest argument against marking, for me, is the workload argument. If teachers are expected to mark every two weeks, and they teach four classes; if each class contains 30 pupils and each book takes five minutes to mark, then five hours of every week is taken up with marking. This effectively means every free period is pure marking. Add on top of this planning, meetings, and other administration, and you have a stressed teacher already.

That is before taking into consideration that most teachers teach more than four classes, and most books take more than five minutes to mark. It is simply unfeasible. More than that, the impact is minimal: in the words of Barry Smith, '30 kids, 3 minutes per book, 10 classes, 15 hours per week, that's 4.30 to 6.30 Mon to Fri, 5 hours on Sat. And what's impact on their work? 18 mins of personalised written feedback per 1/2 term. Approximately 2 hours a year. What's [the] learning return on time invested? What's opportunity cost?'[2]

Marking when nothing else works

I too once believed in the importance of marking though. In fact, I was much taken in by Phil Beadle's *How to Teach*, wherein he writes: 'make no mistake: this is the most important thing you do as a teacher . . . mark their books with dedication and rigour and your class will fly.'[3] Essentially, Beadle contends, you can be the greatest educator ever, but if you don't mark, your students won't progress; conversely, you can be a bit of a rubbish teacher, but if you mark well, great things could happen.

In my first-year-teacher despair, when my lessons were an absolute car crash of poor planning and poor behaviour, I clung to marking. While my mentor and line manager watched me hunched over yet another pile of books ('you're marking again, Jo?') and begged me to instead spend more time planning semi-decent lessons, I plowed on regardless, writing buckets of 'what went wells' and 'even better ifs' on every page a child's pen had reached. I handed books back, and rushed to deliver my next rubbish lesson.

The scourge of book looks, and being wrong

By the time I was a Head of Department, I had somewhat moved away from my 'all marking, all the time' strategy to a more balanced workload, but I still fundamentally believed in the importance of putting marks in children's books. I remember that the week before a 'book look' was always a tough one for teachers, who were noticeably seen with far larger piles of books in the English office, and lugging home bags of books, in the run-up. It was very clear to me who was marking, because I shared an office with them. But nonetheless I needed to collect evidence.

During this book look, as I leafed through the pages of one particular teacher, it seemed clear to me that he had not marked his kids' English books all year. Yet, there was the evidence in front of me – different-coloured pens scribbling advice and encouragement on every other page. But the kids' writing wasn't improving, and it seemed unusual that *every single kid* was ignoring *every single word* he was writing. I asked my line manager what to do, but he just shrugged and said: 'what can you do? The evidence in the books shows he marks. So that's that really.'

Then there was Linetta – fiercely strident Linetta – whose terrifying no-nonsense manner churned out some of the department's best results year after year. She had an NUT flag taped to her desk, and was politically militant on every conceivable issue. When checking her books in November, I found something peculiar. No evidence at all of marking. Nothing. Well – the very occasional scribbled spelling in the margin, or a word underlined. But, brazenly it seemed to me, there was literally one word every five or so books. This was a woman who was clearly not marking her books, and was being unbelievably open about it. Yet, the students were improving their writing. Their writing was obviously better from September to October to November. What on earth was she doing? I decided to dig deeper, and arranged a meeting.

'So, I'm very concerned that these books don't seem to have been marked,' I said, having started the meeting with some niceties about how impressed I was with how quickly her kids' writing was improving.

'They have been marked,' she retorted, her face stiffening, settling in for the fight.

I felt blindsided. This was not what I had anticipated. I stumbled. 'Well . . . I . . . Can you show me where you have marked them?'

She sighed heavily and flicked through one of them. She pointed at a pencil underlining of a word. 'There.'

'I just . . .'

She flicked again. A corrected spelling, in a different book. 'There.'

'It's just that if I can't . . .'

She flicked through another book, found nothing and put it to one side. She was still frantically flicking through a fourth book to show me when I cut her off. 'Linetta, I can't accept that as marking. That's just a couple of pencil marks on a couple of paragraphs.'

'But you said yourself that the kids are improving. Their writing is improving. You said that yourself – *you said that*.'

It was true. I had said that. I'd said that because it was true, but I was starting to realise that I should not have said that. Because if Linetta did not mark her books, we would fail Ofsted. That was what the Head said, that was what my last Head had said; that was what everyone said. I rather needed her kids *not* to be making progress so I could force Linetta to mark.

I swept aside the evidence of pupil improvement. 'The thing is, this isn't the school policy. The school policy is to mark every two weeks, giving a target for improvement. You have clearly not adhered to the school policy.'

'I have adhered to the school policy.' Her face was set and so I could not tell whether she knew she was lying. 'I have marked every two weeks; that is the school policy.'

'But I need to see –'

'You can see their writing! You can see that they are clearly better at writing now than they were before! You can see it, and you said it! Why do I need to prove, to prove *to you*, that they are getting targets for improvement from me? I'm telling you that I give them targets for improvement, verbally, in the lesson, and you're seeing that this clearly works – why is that not enough?'

I didn't really know why. But I needed to get her to do what I wanted. 'The school policy says one target – one *written target* – every two weeks. So I will need to see that in your books in two weeks' time.'

Linetta did not say anything. She stormed out of her classroom, face red, tears in her eyes. She wasn't upset. She was too strong for that. She was furious.

I covered my face with my hands, trying to cool my blazing cheeks. Her kids were making progress. Her results were amazing. Her teaching – what I had seen of it – was incredible. Some kids feared her, but they all worked for her. I suddenly felt like such a pen-pusher, such a *bureaucrat*. Who was I to tell this woman how to mark, when what she was doing was so evidently working for the kids in front of her? Why, instead of forcing her to bend her ways to the school policy, was I not asking her what she was doing, so we could all ensure our children progressed as much as hers clearly were?

I have regretted that interaction ever since, and would like to take the opportunity to set down in print my remorse: Linetta, you were right, and I was wrong.

At the time, of course, this was not how I felt, and when Linetta obediently sat with her children's beautiful books and painstakingly started to put pen to paper, and started to work later, and lug bags of books home, I felt a kind of disgraceful triumph that I now shudder at. What changed about her results? Nothing. But she changed – she became run down, and took more days off sick. She became sharper with children, because she was more tired. She did what I asked, and became less good at her job.

The thing about marking is that we know, or at least we feel we know, that it works – we feel that children do better when their work is lovingly commented upon. But at what cost? And what better things could teachers be doing with that time? Linetta was a case in point: she didn't mark – or, barely marked – and her children were improving all the time.

Issues with marking

In fact, there is an argument to be made that marking is actually *counter-productive*. When we give children the answers, we reduce the amount of thinking they need to do. Remember, kids need to be doing the mental heavy lifting, not teachers. For feedback to have impact, the children need to be doing more as a result.

Which is why the very best feedback is also the most time consuming to give. To help children understand where to put commas, I would write two correct examples in a child's book, and then three more without commas, asking the child to add the commas. Such feedback took a huge amount of my time. If more than one child had an issue with commas, I was writing those five sentences more than once. It was a poor use of my time.

More usual was that children simply didn't read my feedback at all. In my second year of teaching, just at the tail end of my 'mark everything, all the time' phase, a consultant asked one of my pupils, 'What could Miss do to make you act on her marking?' The child replied, 'Read it out loud to me.' When asked why, the child explained, 'I can't be bothered to read what she writes in my book.' I was astonished to get this kind of feedback from a student. It had never occurred to me that my pupils were anything other than grateful that I was spending so much time with their books. Instead, it seemed, they were barely motivated to even read my comments, let alone edit their work with them in mind.

Coupled with the chilling possibility that some children (who knows how many?) don't even bother to read what we write in their books is the likelihood that they actually *can't* act on the feedback we give them. If a child can't use commas, us writing in their book 'add commas' will not result in them using commas correctly. It is unlikely (though, I concede, not impossible) that the reason they aren't using commas is because, although they know exactly how to use them, they just can't be bothered to use them. If a child has failed to include a key fact in their history assessment, it could be because they knew it but couldn't be bothered to write it down. Or it could be that we just didn't teach it well enough the first time. Or they didn't revise it, and therefore they don't know it. Us telling them to include it, without a detailed description of what 'it' is, is of no use. If a child has misused a maths formula, simply telling them to use it correctly is unlikely to result in their using it correctly if they didn't understand it in the first place.

What I'm trying to say is that often we simply need to teach the children again, perhaps in a slightly different way. If one child has struggled with a key fact, others will benefit from going over it again. We cannot be afraid of teaching again, because overlearning key information is beneficial to all pupils, as explored in Chapter 1. Instead of writing a brief version in more than one child's book, which is time consuming, liable to be ignored, and open to misunderstandings, instead we should teach all the children again.

Another issue with marking is the delay in feedback. If, as my aforementioned fictional school dictates, we have to mark every two weeks, for example, then there could be an eight- to ten-lesson gap between feedback. Children looking back on work they completed two weeks ago are unlikely to remember exactly what they were doing. The curriculum will, hopefully at least, have moved on. Even if your feedback is exceptionally well pitched and helpful, the children may struggle to apply it if they can't quite remember what they were doing in that lesson.

What we need to do as a profession is stop pouring time into marking, which is high effort and low return, and instead turn to whole-class feedback. The major benefits of whole-class feedback are that it takes much less time to read children's books than it does to write in them. As a result, you can look at children's books far more frequently. This means they will receive more feedback, and in a more timely fashion. This also means teachers can have more of a work-life balance. For me, whole-class feedback is a win-win.

How to do whole-class feedback

Here's a breakdown of what to do with whole-class feedback. Read every child's book, but just the page or two from that day's lesson (or perhaps two days' worth of lessons at a push). Have a sheet of paper beside you to note common errors, as well as names of children who have put in an especially good effort, or particularly poor effort (for rewards or sanctions). The next lesson, go through your feedback. That's really it.

But let's go into more detail on how this works in practice. We'll start with reading the children's books.

Read their books

When I was teaching 25 hours a week, whole-class feedback meant that I could read each class's books about one to two times a week. I actually often had time to read them more frequently, but I also didn't want to overload them with feedback. It's important the children have time to assimilate what you are telling them. (Sometimes, if I wanted to look at the books more often, I would just skim the last page to give some merits out, especially to the weaker sets, for excellent effort, just to keep the pupils motivated.)

If pupils hand their books in at the end of a lesson, ask them to hand the book in on the last page they wrote on. This will save crucial seconds in finding the most recent page, seconds which add up over a whole class set of books. (I also get them to stack their books on the edge of their row, which means it is quicker to hand them out before the next lesson because they are all in order.) As you skim that page, keep your eyes peeled for things children have got wrong, things children have left out, and, in the 'essay' subjects, spelling and grammar errors.

Try and read the books in a different order each time, but this isn't something to worry too much about. If books are handed in, it is unlikely they will be in the same order each time anyway.

As you read the books, look out for any common errors. At the start, you may not know if something is going to be widespread or not, though after a time you will start to get more of a feel for what each class struggles with. I always note important spellings down the left of the page, errors which will require reteaching (or, at least, explanation) in the middle, and then right at the top names of children I want to give merits to.

Decide what to re-teach

When you have finished looking at books, you may well have a list of 25 spellings and ten things to reteach. This is probably too much for children to take in. I would choose the ten most common spelling errors (or, the ten most vital words that the children have got wrong), and perhaps three things to reteach. Any more than that, and it may start to feel like far too much for them to take in. Use your judgement: a bottom set may benefit from focusing in on just one thing and nailing three or five spellings. A top set might be fine tackling five ideas.

The biggest worry I have heard about this method is that not all children will be 'caught' by this method. That some children make different, special errors unlike every single other child in their class. Have a go – you'd be surprised at how few do *not* fall into the same traps as the others in the classroom have. But yes, you may need to make some concessions to individuality. In a high-ability class, I had an appalling speller – while everyone else focused on the main point of feedback, I would tell him to focus on the spellings – and given that he couldn't spell even basic words, I would have corrected three in his book for him to focus on committing to memory. I also seated this boy at the end of a row, so whenever I was circulating I would go straight to him and give him some more spelling support. In general, I would seat any 'outlier' children at the edge in this way, so you know when you circulate to give them more one-to-one support. Once, I had an early-stage language learner, and after giving whole-class feedback and setting the children off on their improvements, I would make a beeline for him and support him in the very earliest elements of English sentence structure.

Shout-out the brilliant bits

One other thing you might wish to do, though I would stress this is 'nice to have' and not 'need to have,' is to keep an eye out for especially impressive sentences. You can just put a simple asterisk in the margin as you see these and jot the child's name on your sheet. Then, when it comes to feedback, you can simply say, 'Rashida, can you share that amazing sentence please?' She gets to read it out, and you get to explain why it is so good. Alternatively, if a whole paragraph is brilliant, just write the child's name and a 'P' on your sheet, and then pick up their book yourself and read it to the class. Better still, if you have a visualiser, you can project the paragraph onto the board for ease of viewing. (If you don't, you can perhaps snap a picture of it and display it the following lesson.)

Reteaching

Deciding what to reteach and how sounds complex, but, especially in younger year groups, children tend to get the same predictable things wrong, or struggle with the same things. There will be numerous tricky concepts in your subject that the children will find challenging; you will need to become accustomed to going over these. The more experience you have of teaching a unit, the better your teaching will become of these concepts, so over time you may notice a shift in your feedback.

In general, when in doubt simply go over the idea again, but more slowly and with more questioning. At a higher level, you can reteach the idea in a 'different' way, but in reality this probably just means simplifying your expression and checking more frequently for understanding along the way. Encouraging children to ask questions and welcoming them when they do so can also alter the way you deliver the information to the children. Genuinely smile when children ask you questions at this point in your lesson – never show exasperation with them, even if you feel you have gone over this seven million times previously. Never lose patience. These questions are invaluable: they help you as a teacher know what your children need to know; they help you know what they are struggling with.

One further refinement you may wish to make in your feedback is to have a 'stretch target' – not that I would call it that for the children. This is for your highest-achieving pupils, whose work is already accurate and sound in the fundamentals. It could be for them to add detail or complexity to their ideas. With a class with a few outlier high achievers, have a fourth target that is 'if, and only if, you are *sure* you have done the first three. . . .' You may need to monitor this as you circulate, especially if you call it an 'extension' or 'stretch,' as there will be a few who think of themselves as significantly more accomplished than they actually are (and usually some who are oblivious to how good they are).

This feedback may take ten minutes or it may take 30, though 30 is an awful lot. (After a major assessment, you could perhaps give more feedback and more time to redraft; you may choose to use a whole lesson. Use your judgement.) You should use the feedback sheet you have compiled at least one more time, and ideally (in my experience) two or even three more times. After teaching the spellings, for example, give them a day to start forgetting them, and then test them again at the start of the next lesson. Repetition will start to help them to embed the new spellings. Similarly, use the feedback as a reminder sheet for the next piece of writing, so before they begin you can flick back to it and say: 'remember, last time we struggled with X, Y, and Z, so take care to. . . .'

Now, over to them

Now, the trickiest part of whole-class feedback is what you expect the children to do with it. Don't be put off by their first reaction. Classes used to having their teachers lovingly annotate their every thought may well rankle at the thought of doing the majority of the mental 'heavy lifting' themselves. Because what you want, after you deliver your feedback, is for the children to edit their own work themselves, making it better. Some children may claim not to know what to do. If they're a good kid, you might take this as advice to repeat your instruction. But a firm restating of the central improvement, along with a confident walk-away, can let tricky customers know that – no, *they* are doing the hard work now.

Get children to edit their work using a different-coloured pen. This will make it clear to you just how much they are trying. I'd praise those whose improvements show the greatest effort, perhaps rewarding them as per your school's policy with merits or the like to encourage others to do likewise. The visual difference on the page should make it clear what they are expected to do with this time, and feel free to celebrate those heroes of self-editing, along with holding up examples so the whole class sees what the expected standard is.

To assuage their fears over this new policy, make sure you explain in detail why you are doing it. Lean less on the workload argument (I think most children believe their teachers don't have or require lives outside school), and more on the idea that the children need to learn to change their writing and improve it for themselves. This is actually a very intuitive thing for them to understand, because what they are being asked to do now is much harder (actually writing rather than skim-reading your comments), and it is therefore better for their learning.

Another way to resist their resistance is to make self-checking into a habit every lesson. When you finish your recap, get the children to use a different-coloured pen to mark and correct it. When you do short-answer questions, again get the children to mark their own, so they become used to the fact that *they* are the authors of their exercise books. When the children do a spelling test, again, get them to mark their own. (A quick trick I picked up from Joe Kirby was to read the spelling letter by letter and have the children tick each letter as they listened. This ensured the whole class stayed together on the task. You will want to read spellings more slowly for weaker sets, and double check the marking of the very weakest spellers.)

Why I don't do peer assessment

Now, there may be some readers who are thinking that this is an ideal opportunity for peer assessment. Let me tell you why I would advise against this. One of the best parts of students self-checking their own work is that they see the exact mistakes they have made and get the opportunity to write down the correct answer. When students are confident they have got something right, and then immediately find they have got it wrong, you benefit from what is known as the 'hypercorrection effect.' (This is a bit like when you confidently address someone by the wrong name, and they correct you, and then you never forget their name again.) A similar benefit is only transferred to peer assessment if each pupil has made the exact same error, which is unlikely.

The other reason I would counsel against peer assessment in feedback is that it is a bit of a faff. Swapping over books. Dealing with accusations of pupils writing poorly in their partner's book, or inadequately. If one partner is only moderately switched on in that lesson, they can really short-change their peer. If they stick to their own book, they are the only ones who suffer the consequences of their laziness. In general, I would argue that feedback is so precious and so important that it should be delivered by a teacher and acted on by the pupil.

The benefits

The benefits to whole-class feedback are enormous. Not only does your bag get lighter leaving school, your hours get (hopefully) a little shorter, meaning you feel more refreshed and able to teach better lessons. You also – and this is crucial – stop giving out-of-date feedback. You start giving feedback on the last lesson's work the next lesson, and as a result your children are receiving more feedback that they can action. Remember, children can only process so much at any one time. It is very unlikely they will take in *all* your feedback over two weeks' worth of work, no matter how diligently they may try. But taking in three key points on one paragraph they wrote yesterday? This strategy is actually far more likely to result in student improvements.

If you're dubious, try it for half a term with one of your classes and record the difference in their work. Of course, if you do this, make sure you *actually* do it with your class; don't think: 'oh, they're the class whose work I don't mark' and massively neglect them for the other classes. Read their books every two or three lessons, focusing on the big pieces for quality, timely feedback.

What if your school makes you mark?

The final hurdle to this is, sadly, your school's marking policy. Whatever your school, I would save the feedback sheets you have written your advice on. It doesn't cost you any effort to simply stick them in a plastic wallet, so if management turns around and asks what you've been telling children, you can reveal just how many times you have seen their books. Making sure your children edit their work in a different-coloured pen is also crucial to ensuring their books *look* 'looked at.'

But if this isn't enough to satisfy your managers (and, just so you know, it is more than enough to satisfy Ofsted – at least at the time of writing in 2018),[4] then ensure that every time you circulate during the lesson you carry a red pen with you. Try and get something in every child's book, even if it is just a spelling. That way you only need to jot one or two more things in each book when you come to mark them. When you do mark the books, if your school policy requires a written target, write down a letter or number only. Perhaps have your three (or four) targets per class, and for each pupil give them a letter that corresponds to that target. Then, when you give back their books, get the children to write out the target themselves. (If management asks why, say the pupils are more likely to take the target on board if they have written it out themselves. This sounds plausible, and should definitely get them away from asking you to write out: 'use more quotations' 15 times during the course of marking a class set.)

Exam marking

Finally, what about exams? Well, we can't get away from marking exams, insomuch as each question requires a mark. (Although a colleague of mine in the science department experimented in giving students a final mark out of 70, and writing nothing else on the paper. He then went through question by question and the pupils had to work out where they had lost marks. He said this worked extremely well as all the pupils were dying to find out where they had gone wrong.) In any case, you don't need to close-mark exams – it is even less crucial than marking their books, as exams represent the final 'piece' and giving feedback is much more important in the 'learning and acquisition' phase.

Instead, think about which questions most pupils struggle with, and go over these again, reteaching them. If you're really committed, you can write a model answer yourself, but I think it's both nicer and easier to choose the best child's answer and photocopy that for the rest of the class. Feedback on exams might take a little longer, but given the effort the children have (hopefully) put into sitting them, it probably should do anyway.

Marking is one of the most futile things we do as teachers. It is frustrating, time consuming, repetitive, and mind-numbing. Yes, it has its moments, where bright children write extraordinary things, or someone suddenly reveals they can do something they could not before – but you still get these things from whole-class feedback. When looking at how we can get teachers to love their jobs more and stay in the profession, laboriously marking every piece of written work seems like an obvious part of the job to cut out.

Put simply

- Instead of writing out individual targets, reteach the whole class.

- Instead of deep marking every few weeks, skim the most recent page every few lessons.

- Instead of relying on peer assessment, use self-marking to capitalise on the hypercorrection effect and to reduce faff.

Notes

1 The *Guardian* commented on 8 July 2017 that a quarter of all teachers who had trained between 2011 and 2015 had left – some 27,500 teachers.

2 https://twitter.com/BarryNSmith79/status/1046421531100946433 – I've edited the abbreviations that are a necessity of the character limit of tweets.

3 Phil Beadle, *How to Teach*, p. 213 (Crown House Publishing, 2010).

4 www.gov.uk/government/publications/school-inspection-handbook-from-september-2015/ofsted-inspections-mythbusting. Ofsted's myth-buster says: 'Ofsted recognises that marking and feedback to pupils, both written and oral, are important aspects of assessment. However, Ofsted does not expect to see any specific frequency, type or volume of marking and feedback; these are for the school to decide through its assessment policy. . . . While inspectors will consider how written and oral feedback is used to promote learning, Ofsted does not expect to see any written record of oral feedback provided to pupils by teachers. If it is necessary for inspectors to identify marking as an area for improvement for a school, they will pay careful attention to the way recommendations are written to ensure that these do not drive unnecessary workload for teachers.' Accessed 7.10.18.

Conclusion

In my first year of teaching, like many, I worked so many hours – until 10pm most evenings, and both days at the weekend. It was not sustainable. In my second year of teaching, I worked fewer hours – perhaps until 7 or 8 most evenings, and one day at the weekend. Somewhere around my fifth year of teaching, working from 7am to 7pm every day, and at least a half day at the weekend, I started to think: I don't think I can do this forever.

If you are ambitious, if you want to do a great job, if you are a perfectionist – and I suspect many of you recognise yourselves in at least one of these – you will work longer hours than you need to. That is a choice you will make. But any career is a marathon, not a sprint. We need to strip what we can away from our working weeks to make it manageable for the long term. We have a duty to ourselves and to our families, but also to our colleagues and those we lead, to show that this is a job that is not for perfectionists. It is messy and imperfect at the best of times.

I remember talking to someone who said she worked from 6am to 9pm every single day in a school. She was at breaking point. But when I asked 'what could you stop doing?' she had no answer: 'Everything we do here has a purpose. I don't think there is anything you could take away.'

We have to be more ruthless than that. I don't doubt that everything she was doing was purposeful; I don't doubt it was improving the lives of the children she interacted with each day. But it's too much.

We have to be tough on ourselves and take things away, even though they may be good for the kids in the short term. It's hard for perfectionists to accept 'good enough.' One of my favourite quotes, apparently in the offices of Facebook, is 'done is better than perfect.'[1] It is. Finishing your imperfect work, and heading home to enjoy a life outside work is not only healthy, but it will also make you a better teacher. Using your imperfect resource but infusing it with energy and love will make for a better lesson, and having a balanced life will mean you stay for the long term – both things that will directly benefit your students.

I hope that there have been some concrete suggestions in this book that will help readers to find more balance, and to stay in this, the best of professions, for the long term.

Note

1 Sheryl Sandberg references this slogan on a poster in her book *Lean In*, p. 126 (WH Allen, 2015).

Bibliography

Canter, Lee: *Assertive Discipline* (2009 Solution Tree)

Christodoulou, Daisy: *Seven Myths about Education* (2014 Routledge)

Christodoulou, Daisy: *Making good progress?* (2017 Oxford University Press)

Didau, David: *What if everything you knew about education was wrong?* (2016 Crown House Publishing)

Hirsch, E.D.: *The knowledge deficit* (2007 Mariner Books)

Hirsch, E.D.: *Why knowledge matters* (2016 Harvard Education Press)

Hochman, Judith C and Wexler, Natalie: *The Writing Revolution* (2017 Jossey Bass)

Lemov, Doug: *Teach Like a Champion 2.0* (2015 Jossey Bass)

Lemov, Doug, Woolway, Erica and Yezzi, Katie: *Practice Perfect* (2012 Jossey Bass)

Leslie, Ian: *Curious* (2015 Quercus)

Willingham, Daniel T.: *Why don't students like school?* (2010 Jossey Bass)

Acknowledgements

For their generous contributions to this book, thank you to Lizzie Bowling, Christine Counsell, Jon Field, Lucy Newman, Naveen Rizvi and Hilary Samuels.

For their constant support and advice, thank you to Stuart Lock, Carly Moran, Barry Smith and David Thomas.

Thank you to Clare Ashworth at Routledge for masterminding the idea for this book, which would not exist without her.

And finally, my deepest thanks to Sarah Cullen – who, among countless reams of advice along the way, came up with the title.

Printed in Great Britain
by Amazon

66041564R00075